Seven Days in

CAPE TOWN

To Mom, Dad and Grant, with love and thanks

Seven Days in

CAPE TOWN

Sean Fraser

First published in 1998 by Struik Publishers
(a division of New Holland Publishing (South Africa) (Pty) Ltd)

New Holland Publishing is a member of the Johnnic Publishing Group

Garfield House, 86–88 Edgware Road, London W2 2EA, United Kingdom www.newhollandpublishers.com
80 McKenzie Street, Cape Town 8001, South Africa www.struik.co.za
3/2 Aquatic Drive, Frenchs Forest, NSW 2086, Australia
218 Lake Road, Northcote, Auckland, New Zealand

ISBN 1 86872 157 4

Managing editor: Annlerie van Rooyen
Editor: Alfred LeMaitre
Designer: Sonia Hedenskog
Editorial Assistant: Cara Cilliers
Design Assistant: Lellyn Creamer
Cartographers: Mark Seabrook, Desireé Oosterberg and Éloïse Moss
Picture Researcher: Carmen Watts
Proofreader and Indexer: Annelene van der Merwe
Reproduction by Hirt & Carter Cape (Pty) Ltd
Printed and bound by Times Offset (M) Sdn Bhd

5 7 9 10 8 6

FRONT COVER *Table Mountain, seen from Bloubergstrand across Table Bay.*
BACK COVER *Agfa Amphitheatre, V&A Waterfront; Table Mountain cable car.*
SPINE *The* Disa uniflora, *or Pride of Table Mountain, is the symbol of the Cape.*
HALF TITLE PAGE *The blustery winds that plague sunbathers are welcomed by
boardsailers at Blouberg Beach.*
TITLE PAGES *One of Cape Town's most favoured beaches is magnificent Camps Bay.*
THIS PAGE *The silhouette of the peninsula catches fire as the sun sets over False Bay.*
PAGE 6 *The City Bowl is the centre of Cape Town's business activity.*
PAGE 9 *The view from Signal Hill takes in Mouille Point, Table Bay, Robben Island and
the distant West Coast.*
PAGES 10-11 *Home to some four million Capetonians, the Mother City emerges at night
to play and relax.*

ACKNOWLEDGEMENTS

Born and raised in Cape Town, I seem to have been researching this, my first book,
for as long as I can remember. But the face of the city has changed considerably over
the years, and I am grateful to the following people for helping me to rediscover the
Cape Town of today: Rudi and Ivy, for taking me to new places and sharing new
experiences; Brenda, for all the meticulous research such a project demands, and the
many morale-boosting breakfasts it took to finish the book and on time. Thanks, too,
to all my friends and ex-colleagues at Struik Publishers, and especially to Annlerie, my
editor Alfred and designer Sonia, for providing the opportunity to experience what it's
like on the other side of the editor's desk. Most importantly, my thanks go out to my
family, who saw the little boy who chose to read rather than play ball — and
encouraged the aspiring writer and editor to greater heights.

PHOTOGRAPHIC CREDITS

CONTENTS

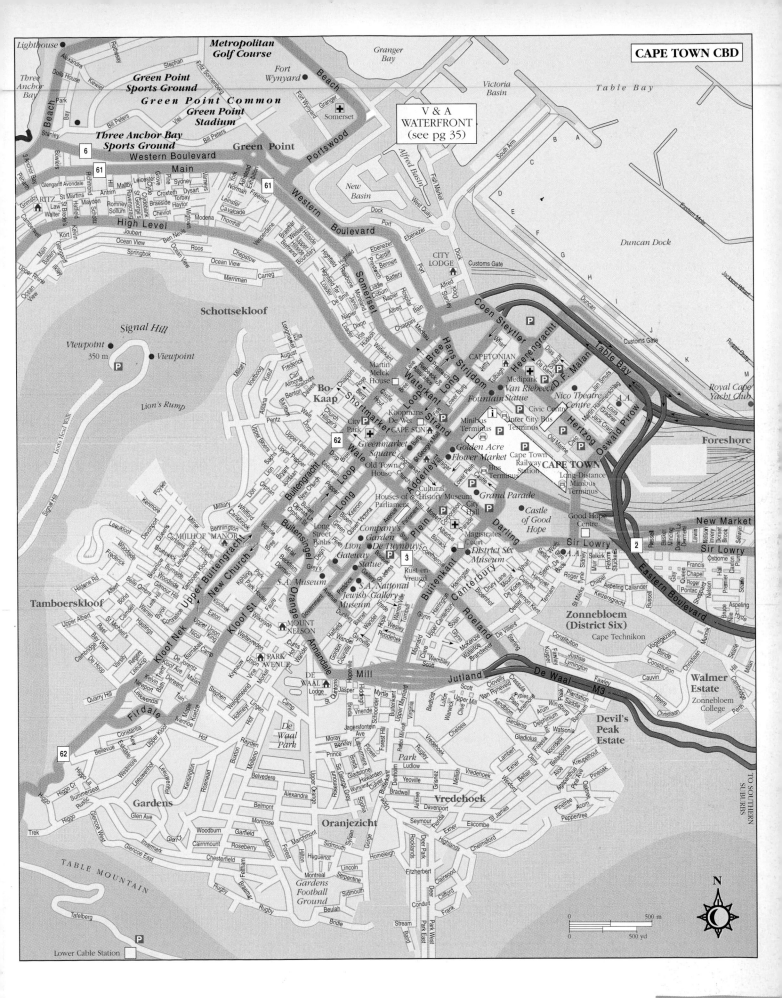

CAPE TOWN CBD

V & A
WATERFRONT
(see pg 35)

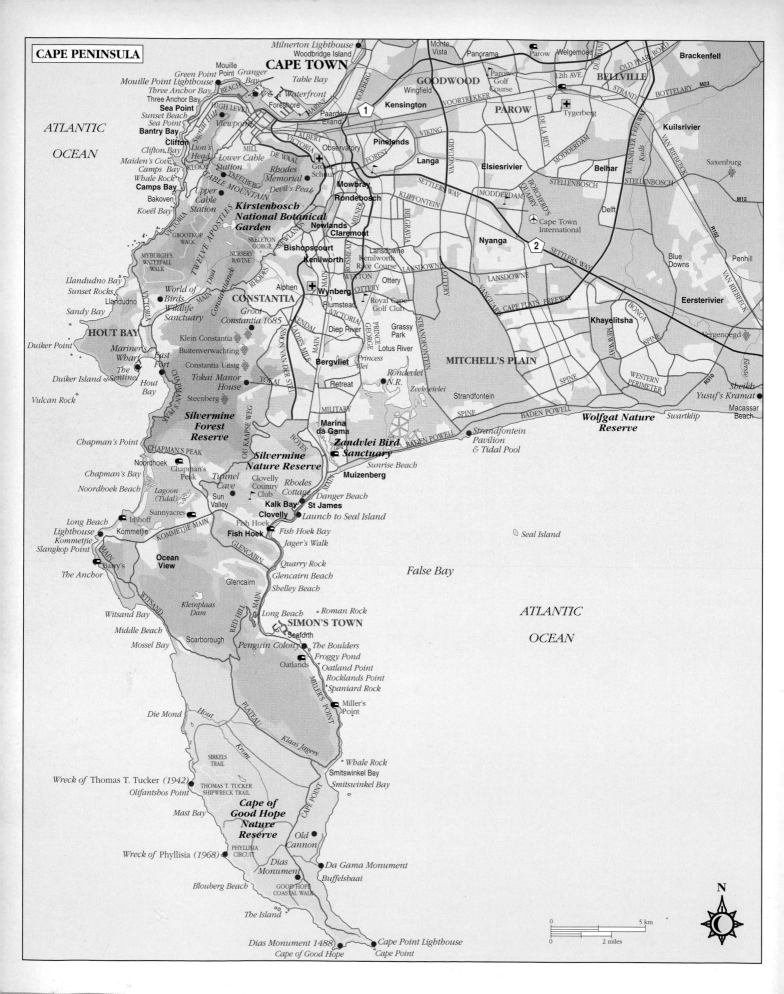

CAPE PENINSULA

ATLANTIC OCEAN

CAPE TOWN

Milnerton Lighthouse
Woodbridge Island
Monte Vista
Panorama
Parow Welgemoed
BRACKENFELL

Mouille Point
Green Point
Granger Bay
Mouille Point Lighthouse
GOODWOOD
Parow Golf Course
12th AVE.
BELLVILLE

Three Anchor Bay
Three Anchor Bay
Table Bay
Wingfield
PAROW
DE LA REY
STRAND
BOTTELARY
M23

V & A Waterfront
Foreshore
Kensington
VOORTREKKER
VIKING
Saxenburg

Sea Point
Sunset Beach
Sea Point
Viewpoint
Observatory
Pinelands
Tygerberg
Kuilsrivier

Bantry Bay
Clifton
Clifton Bay
Signal Hill
HIGH LEVEL
ALBERT
VICTORIA
DE WAAL
Rhodes Memorial
Groote Schuur
Mowbray
Langa
Elsiesrivier
MODDERDAM
Belhar
STELLENBOSCH
STELLENBOSCH

Maiden's Cove
Camps Bay
Whale Rock
Lion's Head
KLOOF
Lower Cable Station
TAFELBERG
Devil's Peak
Rondebosch
KLIPFONTEIN
Delft
M12

Camps Bay
Bakoven
Upper Cable Station
MILL
Kirstenbosch National Botanical Garden
Newlands
SETTLERS WAY
MODDERDAM
Cape Town International
R102

Koeël Bay
VICTORIA
GROOTKOP WALK
Claremont
Bishopscourt
Kenilworth Race Course
Nyanga
2
CAPE FLATS FREEWAY
Blue Downs
Penhill

MYBURGH'S WATERFALL WALK
SKELETON GORGE
NURSERY RAVINE
Kenilworth
LANSDOWNE
Eersterivier

Llandudno Bay
Sunset Rocks
Llandudno
World of Birds Wildlife Sanctuary
Constantiaberg
RHODES
Alphen
LANSDOWNE
OTTERY
Wynberg
Ottery
Lansdowne
Khayelitsha
BONGA
SPINE
Vergenoegd
Fense

Sandy Bay
CONSTANTIA
MAIN
Groot Constantia 1685
Plumstead
Royal Cape Golf Club
VICTORIA
PRINCE GEORGE
Grassy Park
MITCHELL'S PLAIN
SPINE
WESTERN PERIMETER
R310
Sheikh Yusuf's Kramat

HOUT BAY
Duiker Point
Klein Constantia
Buitenverwachting
Constantia Uitsig
Diep River
Lotus River
Princess Vlei
STRANDFONTEIN
Macassar Beach

Mariner's Wharf
East Fort
Tokai Manor House
TOKAI
Bergvliet
Rondevlei N.R.
Strandfontein
BADEN POWELL
Wolfgat Nature Reserve
Swartklip

The Sentinel
Hout Bay
Steenberg
Retreat
Zeekoeivlei
SPINE
BADEN POWELL

Duiker Island
Vulcan Rock
Silvermine Forest Reserve
OU KAAPSE WEG
MILITARY
Marina da Gama
Strandfontein Pavilion & Tidal Pool

Chapman's Point
CHAPMAN'S PEAK
Silvermine Nature Reserve
BOYES
Zandvlei Bird Sanctuary
Sunrise Beach

Noordhoek
Chapman's Peak
Tunnel Cave
Clovelly Country Club
Rhodes Cottage
Muizenberg

Chapman's Bay
Noordhoek Beach
Lagoon (Tidal)
Sun Valley
Danger Beach
St James
Seal Island

Long Beach
Imhoff
Kalk Bay
Clovelly
Launch to Seal Island

Lighthouse
Kommetjie
Fish Hoek
Fish Hoek
Fish Hoek Bay
MAIN

Slangkop Point
MAIN
KOMMETJIE MAIN
Jager's Walk
False Bay
ATLANTIC OCEAN

The Anchor
Ocean View
GLENCAIRN
Quarry Rock
Glencairn Beach

Barry's
WITSAND
Kleinplaas Dam
RED HILL
Glencairn
Shelley Beach

Witsand Bay
Middle Beach
Mossel Bay
Scarborough
Long Beach
Roman Rock
SIMON'S TOWN
Seaforth

Die Mond
Hout
PLATEAU
Krom
Penguin Colony
Oatlands
The Boulders
Froggy Pond
Oatland Point
Rocklands Point
Spaniard Rock

SIRKELS TRAIL
MILLER'S POINT
Miller's Point

Wreck of Thomas T. Tucker (1942)
THOMAS T. TUCKER SHIPWRECK TRAIL
Klaas Jagers
Whale Rock
Smitswinkel Bay
Smitswinkel Bay

Olifantsbos Point
Mast Bay
CAPE POINT
Cape of Good Hope Nature Reserve
Old Cannon

Wreck of Phyllisia (1968)
PHYLLISIA CIRCUIT
Dias Monument
Da Gama Monument
Buffelsbaai

Blouberg Beach
GOOD HOPE COASTAL WALK

The Island

Dias Monument 1488
Cape of Good Hope
Cape Point Lighthouse
Cape Point

N

0 — 5 km
0 — 2 miles

Introduction

$\mathcal{H}$undreds of thousands of foreign tourists visit South Africa every year, and most of these visitors plan a stop in Cape Town, the pride of the southern African subcontinent. Blessed with blue skies, a balmy climate, a rich cultural heritage and a magnificent backdrop of ocean and mountain, the Mother City boasts a profusion of museums, art galleries, restaurants, shops, theatres, night spots and landmarks. Presided over by Table Mountain and skirted by the Atlantic Ocean and a string of exquisite beaches, top attractions include the bustling Victoria & Alfred Waterfront, the famed Kirstenbosch Botanical Gardens, the Cape of Good Hope Nature Reserve, the Cape Winelands, and Robben Island.

Seven Days in Cape Town offers an introduction to these special places, and to many other lesser-known sites and attractions. Seven day tours escort you through the peninsula, covering seven different areas of the city and its immediate surrounds. In addition, the six special excursions take you to the outlying areas, without which a visit to the city is incomplete: the flowers of the West Coast, the Cape Winelands or the Whale Route. Some are best seen over a day or two and visitors may want to stay overnight – especially if the drive to your destination takes up much of your day. A number of routes are suggested, with the street addresses and telephone numbers of the various sites listed for the traveller's convenience.

These scenic routes are best travelled by car – ideal for a leisurely drive and the opportunity to stop and admire the sunset or investigate the unique flora and fauna of the wondrous Cape Floral Kingdom – but areas serviced by regular bus routes have been indicated, and the Metrorail train service runs down the length of the Cape Peninsula. Naturally, special tours and packages may also be provided by the tourist organisations or travel agents operating within the city.

Most of the suggested tours in this book may be completed in one day, but if you're really in a hurry – and prepared to miss out on some of the many tempting attractions – it is possible to tour the entire peninsula in just a few hours.

The final pages of this book are devoted to comprehensive directories that cover shopping, dining and entertainment options in the Cape Town area. Also included is a calendar of annual events for advance planning.

Whatever the reason for your visit, and with all these options from which to choose, it's easy to fall in love with the city of Cape Town. We hope that you will take just seven days – or more, if your itinerary allows – to discover this beautiful city, its people and its culture.

Sean Fraser

Heart of the
Mother City

Day One

HEART OF THE MOTHER CITY

Foreshore and Heerengracht • Adderley Street • Company's Garden • Gardens • Buitenkant Street
Strand Street • District Six • Greenmarket Square • St George's Mall

Running down the middle of what is today the city's Central Business District (CBD) is Adderley Street, the modern thoroughfare which replaced the old Heerengracht or 'Gentleman's Walk', a simple road stretching along the banks of the canal that linked the Dutch settlement to the docks on Table Bay. This conglomeration of Dutch and Victorian architecture, interspersed with modern wonders of glass and concrete, is the heart of Cape Town, and on either side of Adderley Street is an eclectic array of sightseeing highlights and urban attractions that endows the Mother City with its unique flavour.

Foreshore and Heerengracht

The area known today as the **Foreshore** rests on what was once the beach and waters of Table Bay. In order to make way for the ever-expanding city, a considerable expanse of land was reclaimed from the sea in the late 1930s and early 1940s. Reclamation allowed the city to stretch from the City Bowl – the area encircled by Table Mountain, Lion's Head, Signal Hill,

and Devil's Peak – to the new harbour, some two kilometres from its original shoreline. Down the centre of the Foreshore runs the **Heerengracht**, a busy avenue lined with towering office blocks, and dotted with fountains and statues of some of the city's founding fathers. These include the Portuguese explorer, Bartolomeu Dias, and Governor Jan van Riebeeck and his wife, Maria. At its junction with Adderley Street – the upper half of the avenue – stands the **War Memorial**, dedicated to South Africans who fell in both world wars.

Perhaps the most renowned structure on the Foreshore – albeit rather grim in comparison to some of the more recent developments in the area – is the **Nico Theatre Centre** on DF Malan Street. Erected in the late 1960s, the Nico was opened in 1971 and remains the city's most important cultural centre, with an opera house and theatre. As the home of the Cape Town Philharmonic and the Cape Performing Arts Board (CAPAB), the Nico stages an array of local talent in ballet, opera, musical and dramatic productions and boasts a fine restaurant in the shape of **Inter Mezzo**.

PREVIOUS PAGES *Traditional landmark of the Mother City, Table Mountain watches over the twinkling lights of the city.*

INSET *Cape Town's venerable Lutheran Church seems like an island of the past amid the surrounding high-rise cityscape.*

ABOVE *The lively chatter of flower-sellers on Adderley Street is surpassed only by the vibrant colour of their bouquets.*

OPPOSITE *The handsome City Hall on Darling Street overlooks the Grand Parade.*

Hottentots-Holland Mountains

Cape Flats

Southern Suburbs

District Six

Civic Centre

Golden Acre

Castle of Good Hope

Railway Station

Greenmarket Square

Bo-Kaap

Tourist Information

The Cape Town Tourism information office is housed in the Pinnacle Building on the corner of Burg and Castle streets, just off buzzing Greenmarket Square in central Cape Town. This office incorporates the Western Cape Tourism Board and representatives for the Peninsula Tourism Office. The services offered to the public include Baz Bus (a private tour operator which caters especially for backpacking travellers), an internet café, restaurant, and a retail curio shop called African Image. The tourism office is also equipped with a computerized reservation system which offers online bookings for hotels and bed-and-breakfasts, as well as for various tour facilities.

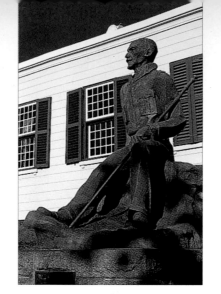

Adderley Street

Named in 1849 for Charles Adderley, the British politician who thwarted attempts by the Crown to turn the Cape into a convict station, **Adderley Street** – the upper half of the Heerengracht – is the city centre's main concourse and forms the heart of Cape Town. Along its busy pavements are shops and businesses of every description, as well as the inimitable flower-sellers and street vendors who add both colour and life to the CBD. Here, too, is a statue of Vasco da Gama, the Portuguese sailor who rounded the Cape of Good Hope in 1498 on his way to India. In December, Christmas lights add a rainbow of colour to the nightlife of Adderley Street.

One of the most imposing structures on Adderley Street is the gigantic **Golden Acre** shopping mall, which was erected in 1978 on the site of the old Customs buildings. As part of the Foreshore, black tiles laid into the floor indicate the original shoreline. Beneath the impressive domed skylight of the complex is a variety of stores, restaurants, cinemas, banks and office suites, but visitors are warned that the crowds in and around the Golden Acre make it an ideal venue for pickpockets and petty thieves. Nevertheless, the parade of pedestrians can provide endless diversion. Within the walls of the complex is also a fascinating peek into the history of the Cape settlement. During construction of the Golden Acre, the site of the original stone dam erected by Governor Zacharias Wagenaer was uncovered, and is preserved behind glass on the lower level. A scale model indicates the location of the reservoir in relation to the plan of the early town.

Historical Cape Town

The **Groote Kerk**, overlooking both Church Square and upper Adderley Street, is the Mother Church of the Dutch Reformed Church (NGK) and dates back to 1700, when Governor Willem Adriaan van der Stel laid the foundations for the new church. The Groote Kerk is noted for its fine architectural and sculptural features, particularly the extraordinary pulpit, which rests on a pedestal of lions, and was carved by sculptors Anton Anreith and Jan Graaff in 1789. The original building was

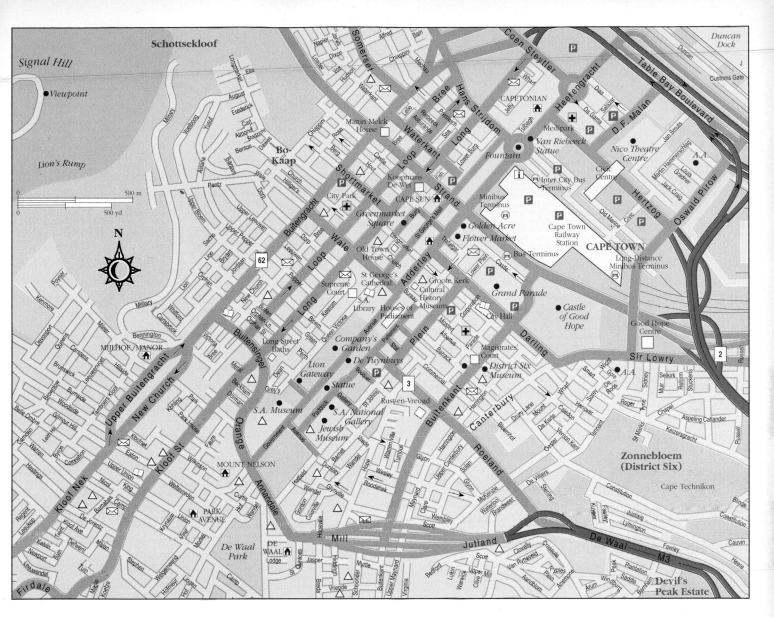

replaced in 1841 by a Gothic-Egyptian structure with vaulted ceilings and plaster ornamentation. All that remains of the old church is the Baroque clock tower and steeple, and the tombstones which pave the floor.

PREVIOUS PAGES *Seen from Signal Hill, the centre of Cape Town spreads across the City Bowl to the slopes of Devil's Peak.*

OPPOSITE TOP *The statue of General Jan Christiaan Smuts at the top of Adderley Street commemorates one of the country's most powerful historical figures.*

OPPOSITE BOTTOM *Shaded by grand old oaks, Government Avenue is a tranquil haven in the heart of the city.*

RIGHT *Grey squirrels indigenous to North America have scurried around the Company's Garden for more than 100 years.*

The **Cultural History Museum** provides visitors with some insight into just a few of the peoples who lived at the Cape during the period of the early settlement. Certain sections of the original Dutch East India Company (VOC) slave lodge – which has served as a brothel and Supreme Court at different times in its fascinating history – were designed by noted French architect, Louis Thibault, and the magnificent pediment on the rear facade was sculpted by Anton Anreith. Museum displays include Oriental art, period furniture, objets d'art (such as stamps, coins and weaponry) and maritime artefacts.

Government Avenue

A line of old oak trees separates tranquil **Government Avenue** from the stately Houses of Parliament, Tuynhuys, the Cultural History

Heart of the Mother City

Museum and the South African National Gallery, making the leafy pedestrian boulevard a favourite both for lunchtime strollers and the animated grey squirrels brought to the colony from North America by premier Cecil John Rhodes. Along the length of Government Avenue lie the six acres of the **Company's Garden**, originally laid out in 1652 by Jan van Riebeeck and his gardener, Hendrik Boom, as a vegetable garden to provide fresh supplies to the ships of the Dutch East India Company when they called at the Cape. Today, the botanical gardens are home to magnificent stands of both indigenous and exotic vegetation.

The imposing seat of South Africa's legislature, the **Houses of Parliament**, is situated on the east side of Government Avenue. The original design by Charles Freeman boasted porticos and pavilions and an impressive dome, which was modified by Henry Greaves to create the Victorian splendour we see today. Opened in 1884, the buildings include the **Parliamentary Museum** and Gallery Hall – containing portraits, sculptures, documents and other remnants of a bygone era. The galleries are open to the public while parliament is in session in the first six months of the year, and one-hour tours are conducted during the periods of recess between July and December.

Next to the Houses of Parliament is the President's city office, the Colonial Regency-style **Tuynhuys**, originally erected in the 17th century to house visiting dignitaries. The building's eclectic appearance is the result of the many renovations carried out over the years. Although restored to its 1795 glory, Tuynhuys is closed to the public, but visitors can stroll along Government Avenue to admire its architectural splendour.

The **South African National Gallery**, also on Government Avenue, is one of the highlights of a visit to Cape Town. The gallery exhibits South African painting, sculpture and crafts, as well as 17th-century Italian masters and contemporary photography. The gallery's permanent collection contains over 6 000 works of art, many of them bequeathed by Sir Abe Bailey, a local politician and businessman.

At the top of Government Avenue, **Bertram House** is a satellite branch of the Cultural History Museum. The red-brick home of attorney-cum-builder John Barker is the city's only surviving brick Georgian house. The museum is a fine example of a British colonial home of the era, and exhibits include superb furniture and objets d'art from the Georgian, Queen Anne and Victorian periods. For admirers of more contemporary pursuits, Bertram House occasionally hosts music concerts, exhibitions, lectures or workshops – covering such diverse topics as painting, calligraphy and flower arranging. For these special events, reservations (through Computicket) are essential.

Fronted on Queen Victoria Street by an equestrian statue commemorating the fallen heroes of both world wars, the **South African Museum** is the country's oldest and most revered museum. Founded in 1825, the museum is today a repository of the cultural and natural heritage of South Africa and, indeed, the world. Lifelike exhibits on indigenous cultures include depictions of southern Africa's oldest inhabitants – the San – which were cast from live models in the first decade of this century. A favourite drawcard are the dinosaurs and other fossil displays. Cultural development is traced through artefacts as

diverse as rock paintings and stone implements to items brought back from the Pacific Islands by Captain James Cook.

Apart from the presentations on archaeology and geology, the exhibitions on Africa's natural history include reproductions of birds, fish and other wildlife. The most impressive of these exhibits must be the magnificent **Whale Well**, which echoes to the eerie strains of whale song while the giant skeletons of these mammals from the southern oceans dangle from the ceiling.

No visit to the South African Museum is complete without a stop at the **Planetarium,** housed under the same roof as the museum complex. This fascinating look into the night skies of the southern hemisphere is so popular that visitors are advised to make reservations for one of the many shows offered daily. Features include a look at the changing constellations of the past, present and future, covering more than 25 000 years. Public lectures explore issues such as new frontiers in space exploration and, for the younger set, there is a talking robotic astronaut and fantastic laser shows.

Considerably more decorous, but nonetheless fascinating, is a visit to the neighbouring **Great Synagogue** and **Jewish Museum** designed by Scotsmen Parker and Forsythe. The Baroque opulence of the Synagogue, consecrated in 1905, is most notable for its impressive dome and twin towers. Alongside the Great Synagogue is the equally impressive Old Synagogue. Of Egyptian Revival design, the synagogue was the first to be built in the colony, and was opened to the Jewish community in 1863. Today, the Old Synagogue houses the historical and ceremonial treasures of the Jewish Museum.

At the top of Government Avenue is Orange Street, which becomes Mill Street to the east and Annandale Street to the west, and then leads into Buitensingel and Long Street. It is along Orange Street that visitors will encounter the elegant old **Mount Nelson Hotel,** one of the finest the city has to offer. The colonial grace of what is affectionately known as 'The Nellie', has played host to royalty, movie stars, statesmen and politicians,

OPPOSITE *The grand exterior of the Houses of Parliament has remained relatively unchanged since the early 1900s.*

TOP RIGHT *The equestrian memorial outside the South African Museum is one of many dotted throughout the city centre.*

UPPER MIDDLE RIGHT *The leafy Company's Garden is the perfect place to take a break from a hectic day of sightseeing.*

LOWER MIDDLE RIGHT *The cavernous Whale Well at the South African Museum is filled with the gentle harmony of whale song.*

BOTTOM RIGHT *Affectionately known as 'The Nellie', the gracious old Mount Nelson Hotel at the top of the Gardens has for decades been a favoured stayover for affluent travellers.*

Castle. Beyond the filigreed iron gates, pillared porch and the Baroque doorway carved by Anton Anreith is one of the finest collections of period objets d'art in the country, varying from furniture to Old Masters, and including a number of works by the noted landscape artist, Thomas Baines. There is also an art gallery with paintings for sale to the public, and a formal herb and rose garden that re-creates a typical Dutch garden of the early Cape.

At the lower end of Buitenkant Street stands the imposing **Castle of Good Hope**, the oldest surviving – and occupied – building in South Africa. Built between 1666 and 1679, this pentagonal fortification, with its stately gateway, was constructed out of timber brought from Hout Bay, stone quarried on Robben Island and lime burnt from seashells. Overlooking the city's Grand Parade – the site of Van Riebeeck's original fort – the Castle serves primarily as a museum and the headquarters of the South African National Defence Force's Western Province Command. Within its fortified walls are both the **Good Hope Gallery** and the **Military Museum** – housing an array of military artefacts and uniforms covering both the Dutch and British periods of occupation.

The five bastions of the star-shaped Castle were named after the main titles of Wilhem, Prince of Orange: Leerdam, Buuren, Catzenellenbogen, Nassau and Oranje. The thick stone walls encompass the original armoury, dungeon, kitchen, barracks, prison, church, cellars and servants' quarters. The entrance fee allows visitors to join hourly guided tours, which take in the lovely **Dolphin Pool**, and to see either the opening Ceremony of the Keys or the Changing of the Guard at noon.

In 1695, a wall boasting an impressive balcony – known as 'De Kat' – was built across the Castle courtyard for extra defence. This projecting verandah facing the main courtyard gives access to the large audience chamber, and is one of the Castle's architectural gems. Inside are fine examples of paintings, decorative arts and period furniture of the **William Fehr Collection**. The displays are of special relevance to the Cape and its history, and are housed in what was once the Governor's Quarters and the council chambers of the Dutch East India Company (VOC).

Darling Street

The **Grand Parade** was once a military parade ground, but is now the site of the country's oldest market. On Wednesday and Saturday mornings, the car park is transformed into a trading emporium, carrying goods such as books, clothes, bric-a-brac and fabrics of every description. The Grand Parade is also home to fruit and vegetable vendors and stalls purveying fast foods – including traditional Cape Malay delicacies. It was on the Grand Parade in 1990 that 250 000 supporters gathered to welcome Nelson Mandela after his release from 27 years in

and remains the epitome of charm and sophistication. Visitors cannot find a better venue for afternoon tea or a light lunch. Although it is rather expensive, the luxury and service remain unsurpassed. There is also a quaint traditional pub, The Lord Nelson, which has been decorated in true colonial style – even the men's cloakrooms have a fine collection of old cartoons!

The **Gardens** area and its immediate surrounds have, in recent times, also become a mecca for connoisseurs of fun and fine food, and a number of highly acclaimed restaurants and bistros have sprung up in many of the old residential homes. For a late-night party and a good meal, head for **Hemingways** at the top of Strand Street, but food fundis should make a special attempt to try the exquisite Thai fare of **Sukhothai** in Orange Street, traditional Cape dishes at **Kaapse Tafel** in Queen Victoria Street and Italian dishes at **Hatfields** in Hatfield Street. The local restaurant scene changes fast, so be sure to watch the local press for details of trendy new eateries.

Buitenkant Street

At 78 Buitenkant Street stands the 18th-century **Rust-en-Vreugd** manor house, which houses part of the historical William Fehr Collection – the remainder may be viewed at the

prison. Mandela addressed the throng from the balcony of the **City Hall**, the Italian Renaissance building of granite and marble on the opposite side of Darling Street. Designed by Harry Austin Reid and Frederick George Green, City Hall was officially opened to the people of Cape Town in 1905; the tower was added in 1923. The hall's main chamber boasts an organ with more than 3 000 pipes, and occasionally hosts concerts by the Cape Town Symphony Orchestra. Bookings for these recitals may be made through Computicket.

Beyond the Castle, on Oswald Pirow Street is the distinctive grey dome of the **Good Hope Centre**, designed by the Italian architect Pier Luigi Nervi. The Good Hope Centre is a popular venue for pop concerts, sport tournaments and trade fairs, such as the Design for Living exhibition held annually in May. Parking here is at a premium and visitors should be warned that car theft is a serious problem and valuables should never be left

unattended. On the other hand, the Oriental Plaza opposite the Good Hope Centre on Sir Lowry Road – which crosses Oswald Pirow – combines parking facilities with colourful stores and mouthwatering aromas.

District Six

Visitors to the city will notice that nestling in the embrace of the mountain is a vacant stretch of land punctuated only by an isolated church and mosque. The **Moravian Chapel** – once a vital mission station for the local inhabitants and now a sports centre for the nearby Cape Technikon – and a mosque are practically all that remains of the once thriving community of **District Six**. Under the apartheid laws, the 'coloured' families who lived and worked in the area were relocated to outlying townships, and the entire neighbourhood was bulldozed to the ground. The empty land was re-named Zonnebloem, but has recently reverted to the original designation of District Six. With the co-operation of its original inhabitants and their families, the area has recently been earmarked for community development. The fascinating **District Six Museum,** housed in the former Central Methodist Mission in nearby Buitenkant Street, continues to document this lost community.

Strand Street

One of the most significant buildings on historic Strand Street – so named because it ran along the 'strand', or beach – is **Koopmans-De Wet House**, a splendid period home that is now

OPPOSITE TOP *The pentagonal Castle of Good Hope, originally on the shoreline, was erected to defend the early Dutch colony.*

OPPOSITE BOTTOM *The cool galleries of the Castle preserve stately reminders of the British and Dutch occupations of the Cape.*

ABOVE *On Wednesdays and Saturdays, the Grand Parade bursts with colour as traders market fabrics and haberdashery.*

Heart of the Mother City

part of the Cultural History Museum. This 18th-century townhouse, with its cobbled courtyard and flagstone floors, was the home of human rights campaigner and Cape socialite Maria de Wet (1838-1906), widow of Johan Kóopmans, who bequeathed it to the state on her death. The house was built in 1701 by VOC official Reynier Smedinga and later renovated by the famed masters, Louis Thibault and Anton Anreith. While it was owned by her family, Maria de Wet and her sister accumulated a fine collection of furniture and household items which may still be viewed in the museum.

Strand Street's other stately old building is the **Lutheran Church**. Because religious toleration was limited in the Cape during the 1700s, Martin Melck opened his barn to parishioners. This humble structure was then converted into a church, featuring a facade by Anton Anreith, who also executed the work on both the organ loft and the exquisite pulpit depicting the Lutheran symbol of a swan. Anreith's facade, however, was replaced by one by Toussaint when the structure was modified to accommodate the heavy roof. Next door to this beautiful house of worship is the home of the resident parson. Today it is known simply as **Martin Melck House**, and this restored – and only surviving – 18th-century Cape Dutch home was, once again, designed by the prolific Anreith.

Greenmarket Square

Undoubtedly one of Cape Town's top tourist attractions, **Greenmarket Square** lies at the intersection of Longmarket and Burg streets. The square at the heart of the city's business district started out as a market in 1710, a place where fruit and vegetable growers marketed their wares, and farmers brought wagons laden with produce to sell to the town folk. Today the quaint square has returned to its original use, and is filled every

day – except Sunday – with funky market stalls carrying virtually anything from clothing, curios, collectibles and crafts to artwork, jewellery, books, leatherware and other fine treasures amid the obligatory curios and tourist souvenirs set out haphazardly across the cobbles. Saturday mornings are packed with shoppers feverishly picking through the bargains on offer and negotiating prices and better deals with bemused stallholders. Although most of the city's open spaces have fallen victim to highrise development, leafy Greenmarket Square, with its open-air stalls and cafés, has retained its earlier role and caters for all tastes.

The patchwork of bright, umbrella-shaded trading stalls heavy with bric-a-brac, junk and, occasionally, genuine antiques, adds colour and life to the central area, and the daily bustle is more often than not accompanied by the sound of buskers. Naturally, prices are subject to discussion, and haggling is part of the passing parade of entertainment. Girding the small square are some very attractive buildings, including the Baroque face of the Old Town House and the beautiful old Methodist Church, built in 1871. Home to the city's first police force, the **Old Town House** – erected in the late 1750s – houses under its star-spangled dome the famed Michaelis Art Collection of outstanding Dutch and Flemish masters of the 17th century, and chamber concerts are held here on Friday evenings. The Gothic Revival style of the **Metropolitan Methodist Church**, with its ornate entrance on Burg Street, is a Victorian masterpiece designed by Charles Freeman.

Church Street

For the bargain hunter or antique enthusiast, the quaint pedestrian mall of Church and Burg streets may offer a rare find. The genuine items are more often than not to be found within the church itself, while the pavements of Church, Burg and Long streets are packed with the stuff grandmother just forgot to throw out. Nevertheless, there may be one or two choice pieces and the stallholders are always willing to help with your purchase of a porcelain plate, Victorian jewel, and brass and pewter knick-knacks. The setting of delightfully old buildings and ornamental balconies is particularly appropriate to the bargaining taking place in the streets below.

Heart of the Mother City

Long Street

The famed **Long Street** – known throughout the city for its magnificent old edifices and charming bookshops – is over 300 years old, and reflects all the allure of a bygone era. Today, Capetonians motor past old Orphan House, where the University of Cape Town held its first lectures, and up the – quite literally – long street, which once saw minstrels entertaining passers-by, and where produce vendors sold their wares from barrows. Today, the street has become the haunt of prostitutes, who frequent its many pubs. Long Street's architectural melting-pot includes Georgian, Cape Malay, Art Nouveau and 20th-century styles. Some of the most striking buildings are the splendid Victorian structures, with their filigreed ornamentation. A fine example is the exquisite Blue Lodge, the only remaining Victorian corner building in the city, styled by Max Rosenberg to accommodate his boarding house. The **Palm Tree Mosque** at number 185 was converted into a mosque in 1807 by Jan van Boughies, himself a slave who had been granted his freedom.

Further up is **Long Street Baths** – comprising a swimming pool, Turkish baths and steam rooms for either men or women (depending on the day) – and a number of unique shops, such as the timeless **Second Time Around**, which stocks vintage clothes, and Cape Town's favourite bookshop, **Clarke's** (for anti-quarian books and Africana). Wander through Clarke's, or enjoy a cup of coffee as you browse through the volumes in the **First Edition Book Café**.

Behind the doors of the 1804 church near the corner of Hout and Long streets is the **Missionary Meeting House**

Museum, which chronicles the Sendinggestig – Dutch for 'Mission Foundation' – established in the early 19th century by evangelists from the London and Netherlands missionary societies to bring Christianity to the slaves. The building contains a fine pulpit, pipe organ and displays on the history of missionary work at the Cape. The floors are of Robben Island slate, while the galleries are carved from indigenous yellowwood and stinkwood, the pews from imported American oak.

TOP LEFT *Buskers who are pinched for pennies entertain shoppers and casual visitors on St George's Mall.*

ABOVE *Acclaimed for its architectural splendour, Long Street is lined with beautifully ornate Victorian structures.*

LEFT *The rhythmic movements of a traditional Zulu dancer in St George's Mall attracts delighted onlookers.*

OPPOSITE TOP *Neat rows of old Cape cottages line the steeply sloping streets of the Bo-Kaap, the traditional home of the Muslim community.*

OPPOSITE INSET *From an unusual vantage point, a young resident provides his own directions to the Bo-Kaap.*

St. George's Mall and Wale Street

The bustling pedestrian concourse of **St. George's Mall**, fringed with shops, arcades, kiosks and bistros, was once a busy city street. Today it is still a hive of lively activity as street musicians provide informal entertainment, and vendors ply their trade. Among the more notable structures is the recently rejuvenated **Stuttafords Town Square**, accommodating the Edgars City megastore. At the top of the mall, on the other side of Wale Street, is the Gothic **St. George's Cathedral**, built on the site of the original cathedral consecrated in 1848, and replaced in 1897 by the new design of Sir Herbert Baker and Francis Massey. This is the home congregation of Nobel laureate Desmond Tutu, the former Anglican Archbishop of Cape Town. The awe-inspiring cathedral boasts the lovely stained-glass Rose Window by Francis Spear, and the 8-metre (24 feet) window depicting early Anglican saints and pioneers. The Treasury houses a list of over 27 000 British soldiers who died in the Anglo-Boer War. The crypt has been converted into a small coffee shop selling light snacks at very reasonable prices. Services are held at St. George's at 11am on the last Sunday of the month, and choral music is regularly performed.

Behind the cathedral is the **South African Library**. Modelled on the Fitzwilliam Museum at Cambridge University, the dazzling white building houses important reference works, including priceless Africana and original manuscripts.

Back on Wale Street, at number 71, is the **Bo-Kaap Museum**. Also affiliated to the Cultural History Museum, the building dates back to 1760 and was once owned by Abu Bakr Effendi, a scholar who published one of the first books in Afrikaans. The house is furnished in the style of a 19th-century Muslim home, with a collection of photographs and personal effects. The museum is also the starting point for walking tours of the fascinating and historically rich **Bo-Kaap** district.

The V&A Waterfront
and Robben Island

Day Two

THE V&A WATERFRONT AND ROBBEN ISLAND

Victoria Wharf · Victoria Basin · Alfred Basin · The Pierhead · Table Bay
Two Oceans Aquarium · IMAX Cinema · Robben Island

In recent years, Cape Town has seen an unprecedented development boom, and nowhere is this more evident than on the shore of Table Bay, the Gateway to Africa. When Prince Alfred, eldest son of Queen Victoria, inaugurated the Alfred Basin in 1860, few could imagine that the simple jetty would evolve into today's Victoria & Alfred Waterfront complex – a working harbour and mecca of shopping and entertainment. The revitalized dockland, set against the backdrop of Table Mountain, is now a leisure wonderland, and has become the country's premier tourist attraction.

Victoria Wharf

Although the **V&A Waterfront** is relatively close to the central business district of Cape Town, it is not easily accessible on foot – walking from the CBD to the harbour means crossing busy main streets. Buses leave roughly every 15 minutes from Adderley Street – next to the railway station – and from The Peninsula Hotel in Sea Point, and ferry visitors to the Waterfront. Whether arriving via the Waterfront Shuttle service or municipal bus, commuters alight at the entrance to the chic **Victoria Wharf** on Breakwater Boulevard leading to the East Pier. The bright and airy glass-topped mall is a stylish combination of upmarket shopping, fashionable eateries and an absorbing parade of both locals and visitors. The complex of converted warehouses houses a cornucopia of fine food, exquisite (and rather pricey) artefacts and elegant designer wear. Also included within its galleries are cinemas, office suites, an automated banking hall and post office. After exploring the mall – be sure to stop for breakfast or a light lunch at one of the celebrated restaurants, such as Morton's, the Hard Rock Café, Caffè Balducci or Mugg & Bean – emerge into the fresh sea air on the other side of the mall. Here, you will find even more coffee shops and fast-food outlets. On the right is the cosy **Agfa Amphitheatre**, an intimate open-air venue in the heart of the complex which hosts a wide variety of entertainers, and is especially popular on sultry summer evenings when the music wafts on the gentle sea breeze. Below, on Quay Five, is a satellite police station, one or two all-night party venues, and an

---

PREVIOUS PAGES *Quay Four and Quay Five in the Victoria Basin form a hub of entertainment at the V&A Waterfront.*

INSET *Age-old inhabitants of the old harbour continue to make their home on the revitalized docks.*

ABOVE *A nighttime panorama of the Waterfront complex shows the new basin in the foreground.*

OPPOSITE *The steel and glass facade of the Victoria Wharf shopping mall echoes the shapes of the warehouses of the old docks.*

Mouille Point

Green Point Stadium

Somerset Hospital

Graduate School of Business

Breakwater Lodge

Portswood Complex

SA Maritime Museum

Waterfront Craft Market

Two Oceans Aquarium

Robinson Graving Dock

New Basin

Cape Grace Hotel

Granger Bay

BMW Pavilion

King's Warehouse

Victoria Wharf

The Table Bay Hotel ➡

Red Shed

Quay Five

Victoria & Alfred Hotel

Pierhead

Victoria Basin

Alfred Basin

The Docks

automated banking service. This is also the docking place for pleasure boats offering charters and trips into Table Bay harbour and along the Atlantic leisure strip.

Markets for Africa

If shopping is high on your list of priorities, however, leave Victoria Wharf via the adjoining **King's Warehouse** on the southwest end of the complex. Food fundis will find stalls purveying fresh fish, ethnic specialities and fast foods. Beyond this lively emporium, visitors will find the **Red Shed**, an eclectic mix of art, craft, textiles and jewellery, as well as an array of traditional African basketware, beadwork, and township art. Of particular note among the more than 20 speciality craftsmen is the glass-blowing demonstration. At the entrance, there is a good fresh produce market. The rear exit from the Red Shed leads to the popular **Ferryman's Tavern**, part of the converted warehouses housing Mitchell's Brewery, which offers a range of beers brewed on the premises.

Market Square and Surrounds

Opposite the Ferryman's Tavern is gravelled **Market Square** – venue for various outdoor exhibitions and performances throughout the year – bordered by the impressive collection of wines at **Vaughan Johnson's Wine Shop**. The selection here is unequalled in the city, and staff can arrange for cases of the Cape's finest wines to be shipped home. On the other side of the square is **Quay Four**, a pub-cum-restaurant nestled right on Victoria Basin. This is a lively spot and the action continues well into the night. From Quay Four

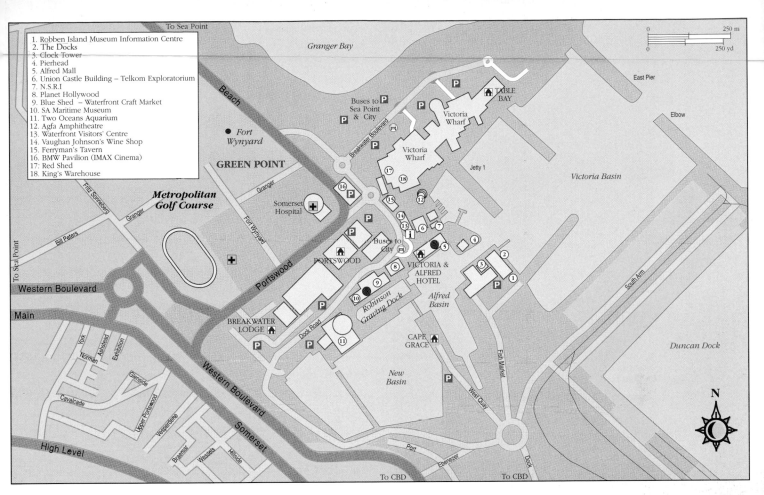

take a stroll to the splendid **Union Castle Building**, to the rear of Market Square, which houses the **Telkom Exploratorium**, a hands-on look into the future of modern communications.

The Pierhead

In your excitement to take in everything the Waterfront has to offer, be sure to take some time to browse around the **Pierhead**, a small extension of the harbour overlooking both Victoria

PREVIOUS PAGES *A gull's-eye view shows the expansive V&A Waterfront and adjoining docklands.*

OPPOSITE TOP *Costumed minstrels with painted faces entertain the crowds at the annual New Year festivities.*

OPPOSITE MIDDLE *The Agfa Amphitheatre off Market Square hosts lively open-air musical performances.*

OPPOSITE BOTTOM *A new swinging bridge links the Pierhead to Bertie's Landing, but the Penny Ferry is a popular alternative.*

RIGHT *Amid the profusion of shops and eateries, children delight in the traditional carousel off Market Square.*

Basin and the entrance to Alfred Basin. This shopping and entertainment enclave offers superb views across Victoria Basin which, in turn, holds the **Victoria Museum Ship**, a reproduction of an old-time sailing ship. The Pierhead boasts a variety of bistros, coffee shops and restaurants. Although there are fewer shops in this little corner, one 'must-see' is the **Coca-Cola Collectables** shop (where the merchandise bears the famous soft-drink logo). One or two of the curio shops are also

Maritime History – The Floating Exhibits

As you walk towards Table Mountain, straight ahead lies the **Alfred Basin** where two floating exhibits are permanently moored. The SAS *Somerset* is the only remaining boom defence ship in the world, while the *Alwyn Vincent* is a vintage steam tug. Both exhibits are satellites of the **South African Maritime Museum**, located just a few metres away in the cavernous **Blue Shed**, which also houses the Waterfront Craft Market. Museum exhibits include the largest collection of model ships in the country, a view of a shipwright's workshop, a children's discovery cove and a shipwreck display.

Hospitality on the Water

Before you reach the craft market, however, you will almost certainly be struck by the much-photographed blue-and-white **V&A Hotel**, which has become a Waterfront landmark. On its lower level, the acclaimed hotel boasts the **Alfred Mall**, which concentrates largely on exclusive jewellery and curios, but also contains one or two coffee shops offering light snacks and refreshments, and the popular **Green Dolphin Restaurant**, which has become renowned for both its fine food and live jazz which is especially popular on Sunday evenings. Recent additions to the Waterfront's complement of five-star hotels are the elegant **Cape Grace** (the Cape Town base of US president, Bill Clinton, during his recent visit) and **The Table Bay**. Together with the V&A Hotel, these are all architectural gems, and the cuisine, vintage wines and dramatic vistas of the Atlantic and Table Mountain offer the ultimate in luxury. Little wonder that they are the chosen stopovers of celebrities.

A variation to the many eateries is the floating restaurant, *Teacher's Spirit of Adventure*, a pleasure boat that offers an exciting evening's entertainment on the waters of Table Bay and surrounds. Back on land is the equally vibrant **Planet Hollywood**, which is housed in the former Dock Road complex. Packed with movie memorabilia, this branch of the world-famous theme restaurant chain brings a glittering dimension to Waterfront dining.

The New Basin

Attractions on the water's edge of the new basin between Dock Road and Alfred Basin include an engaging mix of both new and old. The **Robinson Graving Dock**, one of four working dry

---

worth a browse. Like much of the dockside complex, street entertainers and buskers on the Pierhead provide a pleasant diversion from shopping, eating and walking. These musicians and mime artists – some of them exceptionally talented – add a unique local flavour to the Waterfront complex.

The headquarters of the V&A Waterfront Company is situated in the stately **Old Port Captain's Building**, once the hub of activity in the dock. On the **East Quay** is the restored **Clock Tower** (built in 1887, and housing displays on the workings of the old harbour), and **The Docks** (formerly the site of **Bertie's Landing**, named after round-the-world sailor Bertie Reed), and the home of a popular restaurant and 'watering hole'; be sure to watch for the Cape fur seals on Seals Landing. The East Quay is now also the embarkation point for the official tours of Robben Island run by the Robben Island Museum. To get to the East Quay, visitors may choose to cross the channel known as The Cut (that leads into Alfred Basin) either via the new swinging bridge or by means of the **Penny Ferry**. This quaint water taxi service is more than a century old and the row boat remains as popular as ever, completing the trip in about three minutes. However, the cost is considerably more than the penny it cost harbour staff in days gone by!

TOP LEFT *The charming Victoria Museum Ship is not only an educational experience, but also hosts children's parties.*

OPPOSITE TOP *The lavish Table Bay Hotel plays home to the rich and famous holidaying in the city.*

OPPOSITE BOTTOM *The pristine, modern shell of the BMW Pavilion houses the spectacular IMAX Cinema.*

docks built on reclaimed land, is used to carry out vital repairs to vessels large and small. One of the harbour's most thrilling sights is when sea water is pumped into the dock so that a rejuvenated vessel can float back out to sea. These occasions, however, are infrequent, as ships may stay in dry dock for months on end. It may be far more worthwhile to cross the **Bascule Bridge** to see the majestic Cape Grace Hotel on the West Quay. Beyond this gracious structure there is little of interest for the visitor as the quay leads into the working harbour, much of which is closed to the public.

Back on the west rim of the basin, however, is one of the Waterfront's most visited attractions. The Blue Shed houses the **Waterfront Craft Market**, with stall after stall of arts and crafts, and a boundless array of handwork, curios and memorabilia for the enthusiastic shopper. Although some of the local wares may be quite costly – stallholders inevitably cater for the well-heeled tourist market – they tend to be wonderfully creative and colourful, and offer a little of Africa to take home.

The Two Oceans Aquarium

One of the most popular additions to the V&A Waterfront is the world-class **Two Oceans Aquarium**, a marine wonderland with transparent underwater tunnels, a touch pool and tanks that hold a fascinating array of marine life found along the Atlantic and Indian Ocean coasts of southern Africa. Displays include prismatic tropical fish, a look at the ancient coelacanth, a shark tank, a seal tank opening onto the new basin and the Open Ocean exhibit – two million litres of seawater which is home to creatures both great and small. The aquarium complex also houses a classroom and gift shop, and the **Bayfront Blu Restaurant and Coffee Bar** – be sure to try a unique traditional dish from the unusual selection of 'township fare' on the menu.

Dock Road

From the aquarium, cross Dock Road – the heart of the old harbour and once notorious as the favourite haunt of 'ladies of the night' – to reach the **Portswood complex**, on the southern boundary of which is the **Breakwater Lodge**. Originally a prison, built in the mid-1800s to hold the convicts engaged in building the original docks, the reasonably priced hotel boasts 300 rooms for guests looking for unusual accommodation. The premises are also home to the Graduate School of Business, a satellite campus of the University of Cape Town. Next door, looking towards the ocean, is **Portswood Ridge**, a plush modern development of office suites and a parking arcade. Behind it is the **Portswood Hotel**, overlooking Portswood Road, which leads back into the city.

Directly below the Portswood on Dock Road may be found the treasures of the **Scratch Patch**. Young children – and even some adults – will delight in uncovering the semi-precious stones hidden among the rocks and pebbles. Parents pay by weight for those stones that their children may want to take home. A few steps further on are **Dock House and** the **Time Ball Tower**, once used by passing ships to set their clocks. Buses to and from the city stop on this block, and on Alfred Square directly opposite, outside the Victoria & Alfred Hotel. Across Dock Road is the **Forum Conference Venue** and the **Visitors' Centre,** which handles all inquiries and reservations for some of the facilities available at the Waterfront.

The IMAX Cinema Experience

Undoubtedly one of the most exciting experiences at the Waterfront is the **IMAX Cinema**, situated in the BMW Pavilion on the corner of Portswood Road (leading up onto the highway running into the city) and Dock Road. Projected onto

---

ABOVE *Huge windows and hands-on displays at the Two Oceans Aquarium make it a popular attraction for young and old.*

LEFT *Always on the lookout for a free meal, Cape fur seals are often seen basking on Seals' Landing adjacent to Bertie's Landing.*

OPPOSITE *Since Robben Island was opened to the public, tour boats ferry hundreds of visitors daily to the island reserve.*

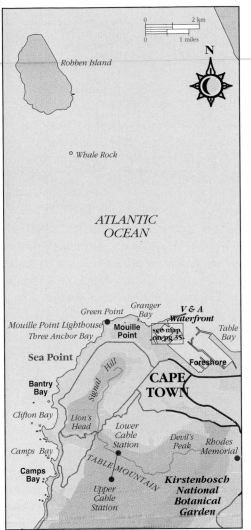

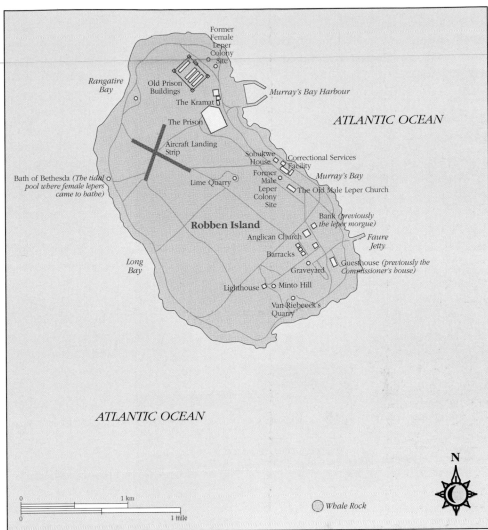

a five-storey-high screen, this Oscar-winning cinematic experience is the world's largest film format, and includes multi-speaker digital sound in a comfortable wrap-around theatre. The approximately 45-minute screenings take place on the hour, but it is advisable to book in advance and to arrive early, as seats are not reserved. It is important to know, however, that the shows run for months at a time, so if you've seen all those currently on show, you may have to wait some time for a new release. The BMW Pavilion also showcases the latest models of the famed German car manufacturer.

The pavilion's **Fascination Café**, which overlooks the busy thoroughfare, serves light meals and cakes, and it also has a limited wine list. It has an upmarket atmosphere and is open daily from 9.30am until 11pm.

Table Bay

With all these enticements on offer, one would think that there is little more to do at the Waterfront than to eat, shop or put your feet up and relax with a sundowner, but one should not forget that the very existence of the docklands depended on majestic Table Bay. Once reserved almost exclusively for maritime trading and industry, Cape Town's revitalized harbour now plays host to a stream of passenger cruise liners, naval vessels paying courtesy visits and even the Royal Yacht

Britannia. Table Bay also features prominently on the international sailing calendar, and it is from here that the bi-annual classic Cape-to-Rio yacht race departs. The harbour is also a major station on some of the world's most prestigious yachting routes, including the Whitbread and BOC single-handed round-the-world races. The premier local round-the-buoys event is **Rothmans Week**, which takes place in the bay in December, and provides a spectacle of colour during the usually blustery start.

On the Waters

Apart from the Waterfront historical walk, details of which are available from the Visitors' Centre, the complex offers an assortment of tours and excursions. Among the most popular offerings from the many charter companies operating from the harbour are round-the-harbour boat trips, twilight cruises, and even game-fishing expeditions and helicopter flights. Quay Four and Quay Five in the Victoria Basin offer boat charters and cruise trips into Table Bay – and even around to Clifton and other spots on the Atlantic seaboard. Particularly recommended are the one-hour cruises around Table Bay, the 90-minute Sunset Cruise and the two-hour Robben Island Cruise offered by Condor Charters. The luxury boat trips depart from Quay Four from 11.30am daily, and their vessels have a fully-enclosed lounge, pub and aft-deck.

Robben Island

One of the highlights of a day at the V&A Waterfront will almost surely be a cruise to **Robben Island**. But be warned that access to this national heritage site is restricted. Most boat trips do not include a tour of the island and it is unlikely that you will be allowed to disembark, unless you take an official tour.

Official tours are conducted exclusively by the **Robben Island Museum**. The 11.5-kilometre (7-mile) boat trip takes about half an hour each way, and the tour lasts about three hours. The fee includes a comprehensive tour of the political prison, and a bus ride which takes visitors to various sites across the island. Ferries bring visitors to the island's **Murray's Harbour**, named after 19th-century whaler John Murray.

This holding place of political prisoners during the days of apartheid has attracted enormous interest since the release of its most famous inmate, Nelson Mandela, in 1990. Today, conservationists are trying to protect the delicate natural ecosystem and unique flora, and preserve the 574-hectare (1 418 acres) island as a breeding place for seabirds. Attempts are being made to have the area declared a World Heritage Site and a national monument. Since the beginning of 1997, Robben Island has come under the auspices of the Department of Arts, Culture, Science and Technology. The prison has been converted into a museum commemorating the liberation struggle in South Africa against the apartheid government.

The history of Robben Island provides a fascinating look into the history of South Africa. Early explorers visited the small

island to stock up on fresh provisions such as seal and penguin meat and eggs. It was also a stopping point for ships, which collected mail left by sailors who passed this way.

A number of quarries are dotted across the island, and these played an important role in its history. There are stone and slate quarries, and two quarries of blue-stone on its beach, but the most renowned is 'Jan's Hole', the quarry from which Jan van Riebeeck collected Malmesbury slate to build parts of the Castle of Good Hope. Seashells from the island were also crushed and burned to make lime cement for the castle. More recently, the lime quarry was the place where political prisoners crushed the limestone used to maintain the island's roads.

Robben Island has served many purposes over the years. Originally, it was the holding 'pen' for livestock needed on the mainland, and went on to become a place of exile for mental patients. Between 1846 and 1931, the island was also a leper colony. The old leper morgue is, in fact, now a branch of Trust Bank serving the 1 200 present-day inhabitants, and the Lepers' Bath – once used by lepers who believed that the salt water

would offer some relief for their sores – is today a tidal swimming pool. Visitors can see the separate leper settlements (men and women were housed apart), and both the cemetery and church alongside the site of the male leper colony. One of the most beautiful structures on the island is the **Church of the Good Shepherd**, designed by renowned architect Sir Herbert Baker, and built in 1895 for use by the male lepers.

Another highlight is the 18-metre (54-feet) **lighthouse**, erected in 1863, which is situated on Minto Hill – at 30 metres above sea level, the highest point on the island. Nearby is also the Officers' Club and, just offshore, the wreck of *Fung Chung II*, a Taiwanese fishing vessel which foundered in 1977. The Officers' Club was once the island's abattoir and is built on Lady's Rock, named after Sister May Harvey, a nun who cared for the ailing lepers and who drowned here in the late 1800s. Not to be confused with the Officers' Club, the Club Building was built in the mid-1800s as the island home of the medical superintendent, and the cellars beneath the impressive Victorian structure still hold the chains with which 'troublesome' slaves were fettered.

An equally fine example of the architecture of the time is the **Guest House**, which was built in 1895 for the island's governor and the pastor, who occupied the lower level. Today the Guest House is used as a venue for conferences.

In stark contrast to these colonial structures is the **kramat**, a Muslim shrine near the harbour and walls of the political prison. The kramat was built over the grave of Sayed Abduroman Moturu, the Prince of Madura, near Java, who died in exile on the island in 1754. For many prisoners, the kramat was a symbol of hope.

Robben Island is dotted with reminders of a more recent period of history, when the defence of Cape Town was monitored from the island during World War II. Outbuildings,

---

OPPOSITE TOP *Visitors to Robben Island disembark at Murray's Harbour, once the site of whaling operations.*

OPPOSITE MIDDLE *The entrance to the once infamous prison compound is the starting point for tours of the island.*

OPPOSITE BOTTOM *Tiny cell Number 5 in the prison's B-Section still looks much as it did during Nelson Mandela's stay.*

ABOVE *Like the fishing boat which foundered here in 1977, many a vessel has met its end on Robben Island's treacherous reefs.*

bunkers and 9-inch guns may still be seen. Varney's Fort – the first lime kiln to be built here – became a power station for the two powerful searchlights used during the war. Of particular note is the Robben Island Primary School, which was built in 1870 and used by World War II soldiers as a clubhouse. Other attractions include the Garrison Church, which still serves its original purpose, and the Old Residency, once home to the local commissioners. The John Craig Hall was built during the war, and today serves as venue for indoor sports and functions. Other modern facilities on the island include a post office, a small shop which serves as the local supermarket, a landing strip for aircraft, and an 18-hole mini golf course.

The natural heritage of Robben Island remains all-important. Elephant and lion roamed here millions of years ago, when the island was still linked to the mainland, but today the fauna consists largely of steenbok, springbok and bontebok, and the birdlife includes a nesting colony of jackass penguins, as well as cormorants and even a few ostriches. The most renowned inhabitants, however, are the seals, after which the island is named – 'robben' is the Dutch word for seals. Because of the human activity of recent years, however, the seals have yet to re-establish a breeding colony here.

Most visitors come to see the island because of its political history, and the fact that it was, for a long period, home to many leaders of the liberation movement. The first prisoner held here was Autshumato, known in South African history books as 'Harry', who was banished here by Van Riebeeck. Another inmate was Makana, who was accused of stirring his Xhosa followers into an uprising against the British in 1819.

The Old Prison and medium-security prison and the administration buildings of the Department of Correctional Services remain, as does the home of Pan-Africanist Congress leader Robert Sobukwe, who was held on the island by

OPPOSITE TOP *The restored Guest House was once the residence of the governor and pastor, but now plays host to conferences.*

OPPOSITE BOTTOM *Warning approaching vessels of impending danger, the island's lighthouse is still in working order.*

TOP *Robben Island's first black lighthouse keeper, Mr Jacobs, surveys the view from top of the lighthouse.*

ABOVE *Many lepers, exiled to Robben Island for nearly a century, rest in the island cemetery.*

government order even after his sentence had expired. Built in 1963, the prison housed mostly political prisoners. It was only relieved of its sombre past in May 1991, when the remaining prisoners were either transferred or released. The most fascinating portion of the prison is Nelson Mandela's cell, which looks onto the courtyard of B-Section. Prior to his election as President of South Africa, Mr Mandela spent almost 19 years in Cell No. 5 until his transfer to Pollsmoor Prison in Tokai, and then to Victor Verster Prison outside Paarl, from where he was released on 11 February 1990.

Table Mountain
& Kirstenbosch

Day Three

TABLE MOUNTAIN & KIRSTENBOSCH

Table Mountain · The Cableway · Walks and Trails · Lion's Head · Signal Hill
Devil's Peak · Kirstenbosch National Botanical Garden

For decades, the famed flat-topped mountain which forms the backdrop to the city of Cape Town – with Kirstenbosch Botanical Gardens on its eastern slopes – has enjoyed unparalleled status as the country's top tourist attraction. Today, both the mountain and the world-renowned gardens continue to attract more than two million visitors a year, second only to the Victoria & Alfred Waterfront on the docklands of Table Bay.

Flanked by Devil's Peak and Lion's Head, monolithic **Table Mountain** – which can be spotted from as far as 200 kilometres (124 miles) out at sea – was given its rather apt name by Portuguese explorer and adventurer Antonio de Saldanha. The impressive hulk of shale, sandstone and granite – Maclear's Beacon is the mountain's highest point – towers 1 086 metres (3 564 feet) above the city's shoreline, and its characteristic flat surface extends almost three kilometres, making it the country's most familiar landmark. At night, the front of the mountain is lit by floodlights, which give its imposing ramparts an even more romantic quality.

The Cableway

Virtually every visitor to Cape Town's shores seems determined to venture to the summit of the mountain, and the old cableway which has been in service since early this century saw heavy traffic. For this reason, the Table Mountain Aerial Cableway Company recently renovated and upgraded the existing facilities so that visitors may enjoy a faster and more efficient service.

In operation since October 1997, the new cable car departs from the cable station at the top of Kloof Nek Road and takes five minutes to complete the trip to the summit. Visitors who do not have their own transport to the cable station may take a taxi or the bus which leaves every 30 minutes from both the Grand Parade bus depot or from the OK Bazaars store on Adderley Street. Queues can be expected during peak tourist season, but the wait to board the cable car is generally brief.

The new cable car takes as many as 65 people at a time, and operates virtually throughout the year – depending, of course, on Cape Town's somewhat erratic weather conditions. The

---

PREVIOUS PAGES *The much-photographed flat-topped landmark that symbolizes the Mother City, seen from Bloubergstrand.*

INSET *Rock hyrax, or dassies, may be seen cavorting among the rocks at the summit of Table Mountain.*

ABOVE *A chattering sugarbird pauses on one of Kirstenbosch's crane-like strelitzias.*

OPPOSITE *Dramatic lookout points atop Table Mountain afford exhilarating views of the city and its environs.*

False Bay

Cape Point

Muizenberg

Table Mountain

Devil's Peak

Castle of Good Hope

Foreshore

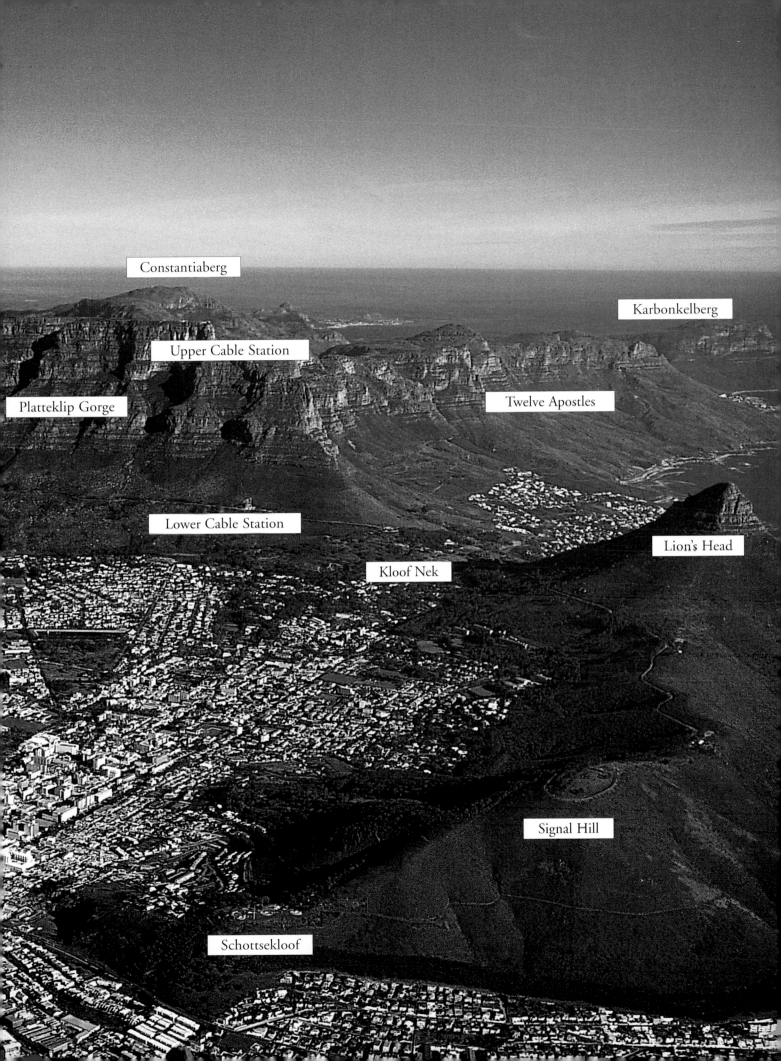

Constantiaberg

Karbonkelberg

Upper Cable Station

Platteklip Gorge

Twelve Apostles

Lower Cable Station

Lion's Head

Kloof Nek

Signal Hill

Schottsekloof

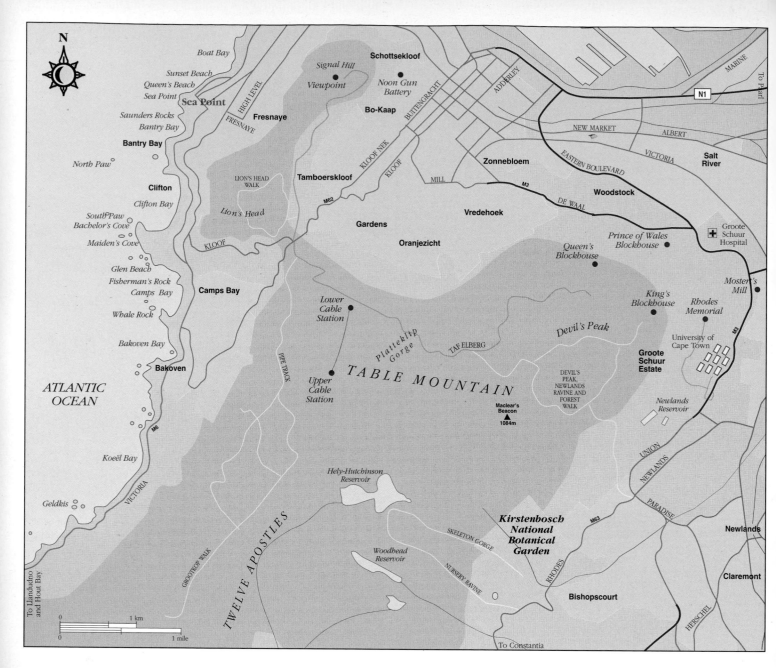

ascent, on the other hand, is well worth any time spent in a queue, and the view of the peninsula and surrounds from the summit is reward enough. Apart from the breathtaking panorama, perhaps the most impressive sight on Table Mountain is its unique array of flora and fauna. Scurrying among the rocks and shrubs are rock hyrax – known locally as dassies – which have inhabited the mountain slopes since long before human settlement. These fascinating little creatures, with their shining black eyes and short-haired coats are, despite their rodent-like appearance, related to the elephant, and are found on many of the high-lying, mountainous areas of the Cape.

Floral Fantasy

Table Mountain, with its spectacular assortment of vegetation, forms a vital part of the Cape Floral Kingdom, which includes more than 8 500 plants, flowers, trees and shrubs – comprising virtually all of the peninsula's indigenous floral heritage. The unique natural habitat of hardy, evergreen vegetation known as fynbos (from the Afrikaans word meaning 'fine bush'), the peak

flowering season sees nearly 1 500 species of plants erupt in colour and texture. Floral gems include ericas, proteas – including the king protea, South Africa's national flower – and disas, the most familiar of which is the red *Disa uniflora*, also known as the Pride of Table Mountain, and the provincial emblem of the Western Cape. A standout among tree species is the majestic silver tree, with its distinctive silver-grey foliage.

A World Apart

The cableway restaurants are operated by **Café Paradiso**, a popular Mediterranean-style eatery located on trendy Kloof Street. For those visitors who may have chosen to walk up the slopes and are in need of sustenance, the summit boasts a bistro serving light lunches and other refreshments, and a much-expanded licensed restaurant constructed from the mountain's own sandstone. There is also a souvenir outlet which stocks postcards and books, and even a fax and postal service – a letter will bear the prized postmark indicating that it was posted from the top of Table Mountain. There is also a relief model of the Cape Peninsula which pinpoints landmarks and places of special interest, and provides a useful point of orientation.

PREVIOUS PAGES *Majestic Table Mountain forms part of a chain of mountains reaching southward to distant Cape Point.*

OPPOSITE *Captured in a scale model situated at the top of the mountain, the peninsula invites visitors to explore its treasures.*

ABOVE *A network of gentle footpaths guides walkers to view-sites and points of interest around the summit of Table Mountain.*

Walking the Mountain

With a spectacular view across the **Twelve Apostles** – there are, in fact, 17 peaks in this range – to Cape Point, the mountain is popular with both serious hikers and casual amblers. The latter may prefer to stroll along the Tortoise, Rock Dassie or Klipspringer walks – short demarcated summit trails that range in duration from five to 30 minutes. Climbers should always be accompanied by either a group of companions or a recognised guide. All too often, climbers have either lost their way or fallen victim to the mountain's many cliffs and precipices. Should you wish to arrange an organised venture into the rocky terrain, contact the **Mountain Club of South Africa**, or the **Tourism Gateway**, who can provide details about guides.

Table Mountain boasts about 300 different walks which vary in distance and demand various degrees of both stamina and fitness. Apart from a guide, climbers should also wear suitable climbing shoes or boots, plan for both extremes of weather, pack enough food, water and emergency supplies and, most importantly, stick to the assigned footpaths. Officials also recommend that climbers take along a cellular telephone if possible, and also let friends or family members know where they will be walking and when they expect to return.

Climbing the Mountain

A number of maps detail most of the walking and climbing routes on the mountain, and may prove handy – if not necessary – to climbers. Maps are available from the shop at the top of the mountain, and outlets such as those at Kirstenbosch Botanical Gardens and other city souvenir shops.

The **Platteklip Gorge** walk on the Kloof Nek side of the mountain extends between the two cableway stations, and is a relatively trouble-free stroll which should take about 2.5 hours

to complete. The **Contour Path** follows the contour line from majestic Rhodes Memorial directly to Kirstenbosch – in about two to three hours – from where hikers may walk to both Cecilia Ravine and Cecilia Forest in the suburb of Newlands. An alternative route is the circular walk from the front of the mountain to the Woodhead and Hely-Hutchinson dams and the Waterworks Museum which houses the history of the two reservoirs. Yet another choice may be to walk up Nursery Ravine from Kirstenbosch to the Woodhead Dam, and then down Cecilia Ravine. The definitive guidebook to the many trails of Table Mountain is Colin Paterson-Jones's *Table Mountain Walks* (Struik Publishers, 1991).

Lion's Head

To the west of Table Mountain rears **Lion's Head**, from the base of which extends Signal Hill. For keen climbers, Lion's Head provides something of a challenge and casual hikers should note that it is not all level ground and pleasant strolling. Metal ladders and chains have been inserted into the rock face to assist climbers to reach the top of the 669-metre (2 195 feet) peak. Although not gruelling, the climb requires some degree of effort. A pleasant alternative, however, is to drive along Signal Hill. The brightly painted **kramat** visible from the road is one of many shrines dotted around the Cape Peninsula to honour Islamic leaders. Members of the Cape's large Muslim community believe that these shrines watch over and protect the citizens of Cape Town. Visitors are welcome, but are reminded that dress should be appropriate to the holy ground, and that it is polite to leave your shoes at the door.

Signal Hill

Signal Hill, the mountainous knoll that divides the city from Sea Point and beyond, looks across exclusive residential suburbs such as Bantry Bay and a spectacular strip of white beaches. At the end of the summit drive is a parking area, viewing point and picnic facilities. Of course, Signal Hill is famous not only as one of the best vantage points from which to watch the sunset, but also as the site of the **noon gun**. This old naval cannon is fired every day of the week (except Sundays) from a battery on Schottsekloof just below the summit of Signal Hill, and the sound reverberates throughout the City Bowl. Formerly fired from the grounds of the Castle of Good Hope, the noon

TOP LEFT *The rotating floor of the shiny new cable car affords visitors a 360° view of the mountain slopes and the city below.*

TOP RIGHT *The kramat on Signal Hill is a shrine to the Muslim missionary, Sheikh Mohamed Hassen Ghaibie Shah.*

ABOVE *The echoing boom of the noon gun has signalled midday since the earliest days of the settlement.*

OPPOSITE TOP *Wisps of the cloud so aptly named The Table Cloth drift past the bulk of Lion's Head.*

OPPOSITE BOTTOM *On a clear day, paragliders relish the thrill of a bird's eye view of the mountain and city below.*

gun signals midday, but also serves as a reminder of those who lost their lives during the two world wars. In days gone by, flags were also raised here so that the town could get ready for the arrival of ships in Table Bay.

Devil's Peak

On the slopes of Devil's Peak, on the eastern side of Table Mountain, are three blockhouses built by British troops during the second British occupation of the Cape (1806). The **Queen's Blockhouse** still stands and has been faithfully restored, but only rubble remains of the **Prince of Wales Blockhouse**. Of the three, the most impressive is the **King's Blockhouse**, formerly a prison and today a historical monument. There is little else on the slopes of Devil's Peak, yet the 1 002-metre (3 288 feet) peak remains a popular hiking destination. It should, however, be tackled only by experienced climbers and, even then, in the company of a guide familiar with the mountain trails.

Kirstenbosch

The **National Botanical Garden** at Kirstenbosch is run by the National Botanical Institute, and the information office at the main entrance provides a wealth of material on the present, past and future of this imposing wonderland, known throughout

the world for its spectacular beauty and incredible diversity of plants. Known informally as Kirstenbosch, the gardens spread across the mountain's eastern slopes and extend up to Maclear's Beacon. There is an entrance fee. There is ample free parking, and bus services run to and from the railway stations at Mowbray and nearby Claremont.

The People's Garden

On his death in 1902, Cecil John Rhodes – whose memorial stands on the lower slopes of Devil's Peak – left the grounds of Kirstenbosch to the South African people, and the gardens were formally established in 1913. Today, Kirstenbosch comprises over 500 hectares (1 235 acres), as well as 478 hectares (1 181 acres) of fynbos and natural forest. The landscape includes nearly 7 000 species of indigenous plants, nearly 1 000 of which occur naturally within the area – many are unique to the slopes of Table Mountain. Some 36 hectares (89 acres) are reserved solely for cultivation and research.

The Compton Herbarium

Originally situated within the perimeter of the gardens, the **Compton Herbarium** was recently moved to nearly five hectares (12 acres) of ground bought from the City of Cape

Scientists and educators have also established the Goldfields Environmental Education Centre. The centre provides outings for school groups and other interested parties, and also holds lectures on the wildlife of southern Africa.

Birdsong

As may be expected in such a natural wonderland, the birdlife is prolific. The information office stocks checklists of those species which may be spotted within the confines of the gardens, and Colin Paterson-Jones's *Visitor's Guide to Kirstenbosch* may prove essential reading on both the wildlife and the story of these beautiful gardens. This handy book is available from The Garden Shop at the main gate, which also stocks books on the country, small gifts and mementoes, and a wide selection of indigenous plants.

An added attraction of the gardens is the popular summertime concerts. Flocks of music lovers congregate on the lawns to enjoy an eclectic repertoire ranging from classical and choral music to the vibrant sounds of local pop bands.

Sadly the old Kirstenbosch Tea House, a favourite spot among Capetonians for afternoon tea, breakfast and Sunday lunch, was closed in the course of 1999.

In 1998, Kirstenbosch opened a new **visitors' centre**, located near the main entrance off Rhodes Drive. The complex provides access to the impressive new stone and glass **conservatory**. More commonly known as the Glass House, the conservatory displays arid-adapted and alpine species that require specific moisture and temperature conditions and so cannot be displayed out of doors. The centrepiece of the new facility is a large baobab tree that was brought to Kirstenbosch from the Northern Province.

Kirstenbosch Craft Market

The last Sunday of every month (except June to August) sees the ever-popular Kirstenbosch Craft Market spread across the grass verges of the gardens below the main gate on Rhodes Drive. The market has developed into a meeting place for fine crafters from throughout the peninsula, who offer a dizzying

---

TOP LEFT *Among the fynbos species of the Cape Floral Kingdom that are found in Kirstenbosch are ericas, pictured here.*

MIDDLE LEFT *The delicate blooms of the pincushion protea may vary from soft yellow to dusky pink.*

BOTTOM LEFT *Robust and strong, the majestic king protea represents one of the garden's most prolific plant species.*

OPPOSITE *With its burst of colour and unrivalled mountain backdrop, Kirstenbosch is one of the world's most beautiful botanical gardens.*

Town. The herbarium was named in 1919 for RH Compton, the director of the National Botanical Gardens under whose auspices the *Journal of South African Botany* would eventually be launched in 1935. The facility has now extended its original function to include a research centre and laboratory dealing largely with the scientific aspects of the country's extensive plant life. Today, the research centre – which is closed to the public – houses nearly half a million botanical specimens, and its botanists work with colleagues throughout the world in order to study and protect the natural heritage of the region.

array of goods ranging from traditional sculptures, beadwork and weaving to ceramics, jewellery and clothing. There are also food stalls offering sweet or savoury delights. All the goods on offer are of a very high quality, as the Botanical Society – under whose auspices the market is run – keeps a tight control on marketers who apply for the limited space available. Only hand-crafted wares may be sold here, and the craftsperson must be on hand to serve his or her customers. As a result, the Kirstenbosch Craft Market has developed an enviable reputation as the standout among the city's many informal weekend markets.

Walks through Kirstenbosch

Many visitors to Kirstenbosch are keen to traverse the mountain landscape, and several trails lead up the mountain slopes from the gardens. As with any walk or climb through unfamiliar territory, visitors are urged to take precautions and to plan their walk with the aid of maps and guides. The many reliable footpaths offer dramatic views and provide ideal routes, and should be adhered to at all times. Should you require a guide, enquire at the main gate, and expect to pay a small fee for the assurance of personal safety.

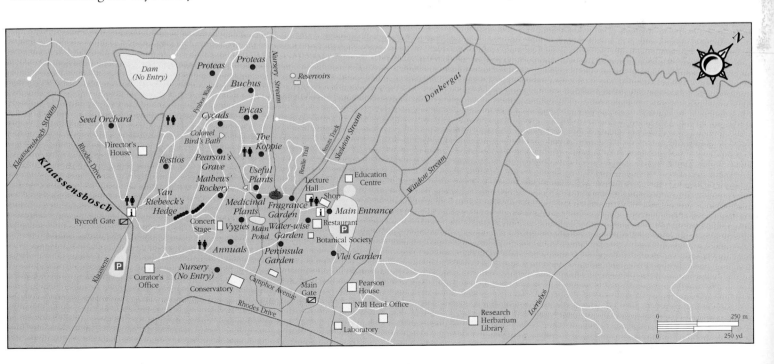

The Dell and Cycad Amphitheatre

Nestled in the Dell below the famed Cycad Amphitheatre is a bird-shaped well fed throughout the year by the springs which flow into it. Edged with stones brought to the Cape from Batavia, the pool is known – albeit mistakenly – as Lady Anne Barnard's Bath, in reference to the wife of Andrew Barnard, the secretary to the governor, Earl Macartney, who acted as First Lady and official hostess during her stay at the Cape. The bath itself is, in fact, called **Colonel Bird's Bath**, after Colonel Christopher Bird, the civil servant who built it in about 1811 – some years after Lady Anne left the shores of the Cape!

The area surrounding the bath boasts not only all four of the country's indigenous yellowwood tree species, but also the only Cape species of holly *Ilex mitis*, and of course, the **Cycad Amphitheatre**. These non-flowering, seed-bearing plants, ranged up the steep slope, belong to an ancient order of plants that flourished many millions of years ago. Although cycads bear some resemblance to palm trees, they are in fact unrelated. Cycads were among the first species planted in the newly established Kirstenbosch by the garden's first director, Professor Harold Pearson, in 1903. Pearson's grave, alongside the collection of cycads, is watched over by an enormous blue Atlas cedar shipped from Kew Gardens in London.

Mathews' Rockery

A collection of mostly succulents from southern Africa's arid regions, the **Mathews' Rockery** was initiated by the gardens' first curator, JW Mathews, who began putting together the sandstone rockery in 1927. In addition to the sometimes bizarre shapes of the succulents, the garden, however, also boasts an assortment of bulb flowers and other plants, such as aloes, which erupt in colour during the winter months. From the path leading to both the rockery and the Dell, visitors may still see portions of Jan van Riebeeck's **wild almond hedge**, which marked the boundary of the very first European settlement at the Cape.

Pelargonium Koppie and Environs

Home to the colourful pelargoniums, **Pelargonium Koppie** abounds with dry fynbos species. Along the footpath through the area is also the aromatic **herb garden**, a popular stopping point at which to see the rooibos and honey tea bushes – often used to brew herbal tea – which grow here. All the plants' parts are combined to create fragrant perfumes, food flavouring and home medicines.

A fascinating diversion for the visitor is the aptly named **Fragrance Garden** opposite the herb garden. While the plants display interesting hues of grey, blue and green, the air here is thick with the aroma of scented leaves which almost beg to be touched, felt and smelled. The informative signs are printed in large type, with Braille provided for the benefit of sight-impaired visitors. The information provided is both interesting and informative, and invites the reader to follow the half-kilometre **Braille Trail** nearby. A rope guides visitors to the approximately 10 stopping points at which further descriptions and details are provided in Braille and print.

ABOVE *With more than 500 hectares (1 235 acres) of verdant terrain, Kirstenbosch offers many corners of solitary beauty.*

OPPOSITE TOP *The intoxicating scents of the Fragrance Garden are an endless delight to children and adults alike.*

OPPOSITE BOTTOM *The baobab in the conservatory at the visitors' centre was brought in from the Northern Province.*

The Camphor Avenue

Originally home to the Compton Herbarium mentioned earlier, the camphor trees which line this route were introduced by the Cape premier and businessman Cecil Rhodes, when the avenue still served as part of the main road between Newlands and Hout Bay. The area surrounding this exotic avenue of trees boasts an array of cycads and vibrantly coloured flowers, while the new Botanical Society Conservatory lies directly opposite.

Fynbos

The paved **Fynbos Walk** extends from Rycroft Gate to Pelargonium Koppie, along the higher slopes of Kirtsenbosch's cultivated section. Near the gate are gardens devoted to the three most prominent fynbos groups – restio, protea and erica. Among the botanical curiosities to be found in the restio garden are reeds which are said to live for up to 60 years – and beyond, say some – while the erica garden is a constant parade of colour as the 600 different species bloom one after the other throughout the year. The protea garden, with its characteristic subdued shades, is at its best in late March and early April, while the garden's leucadendrons and silver trees – the six-kilometre (3.7 miles) forest trail shows these at their finest – bloom in spring. Summer is the turn of the pincushions.

Table Mountain & Kirstenbosch

The Atlantic
Seaboard

Day Four

THE ATLANTIC SEABOARD

Green Point • Mouille Point • Three Anchor Bay & Sea Point • Bantry Bay • Clifton • Camps Bay
Bakoven • Oudekraal • Llandudno • Sandy Bay • Suikerbossie • Hout Bay • Chapman's Peak Drive • Noordhoek

The strip of the peninsula's shoreline commonly known as the Atlantic Seaboard stretches some 55 kilometres (34 miles) from the waters of Table Bay along the western coast to the nature reserve at Cape Point. The exceptional beaches and rugged mountains along this coastline not only make this a popular drive – for both locals and visitors – but also provide outstanding views across the Atlantic Ocean, with some of the most spectacular sunsets in the world. Naturally, the plush homes along this coast sell for millions.

Green Point

On the slopes above the Victoria & Alfred Waterfront and Table Bay is the seaside suburb of **Green Point**. Along with Sea Point, Green Point became home to well-heeled segments of Cape society in the 1940s and 1950s. With the development of the seafront, many of the area's numerous apartment blocks are in demand once again as South Africans and wealthy foreign investors clamour for the sea views. As expected, the few hotels here are equally exclusive.

Visitors leaving the Waterfront from the Green Point exit will immediately encounter a majestic old building resembling a fort. This is the century-old New Somerset Hospital which houses the **Cape Medical Museum**. The museum's displays reflect the early days of medical treatment – particularly the dental practices of Victorian society. One of the more curious exhibits is the photograph of James Barry, the first physician to carry out a Caesarian section in the country. Upon his death, or so it is rumoured, Barry was discovered to be a woman.

Alongside Somerset Hospital stretch the grassy fairways of Green Point's Metropolitan Golf Course, and behind is **Green Point Stadium**. Encircled by a large parking lot, the concrete stadium is the home ground of local soccer teams Cape Town Spurs, Hellenic and Santos, but is also home base of the annual **Coon Carnival**. Held at New Year, the festival sees minstrels from the Cape's coloured community don colourful costumes and parade to the vibrant sounds of musicians and singers.

Green Point Stadium has, in recent years, also become a favoured venue for the many international pop stars and music

PREVIOUS PAGES *With the Atlantic at its calmest, the last rays of the setting sun cast a warm glow over Sea Point.*

INSET *Glorious sunny summer days make the palm-fringed beach at Camps Bay the place to see and be seen.*

ABOVE *With a laid-back vibe reminiscent of Los Angeles, the Sea Point Promenade is popular with both joggers and walkers.*

OPPOSITE *Famed throughout the country – and increasingly abroad – Clifton's idyllic Fourth Beach is a sunbather's heaven.*

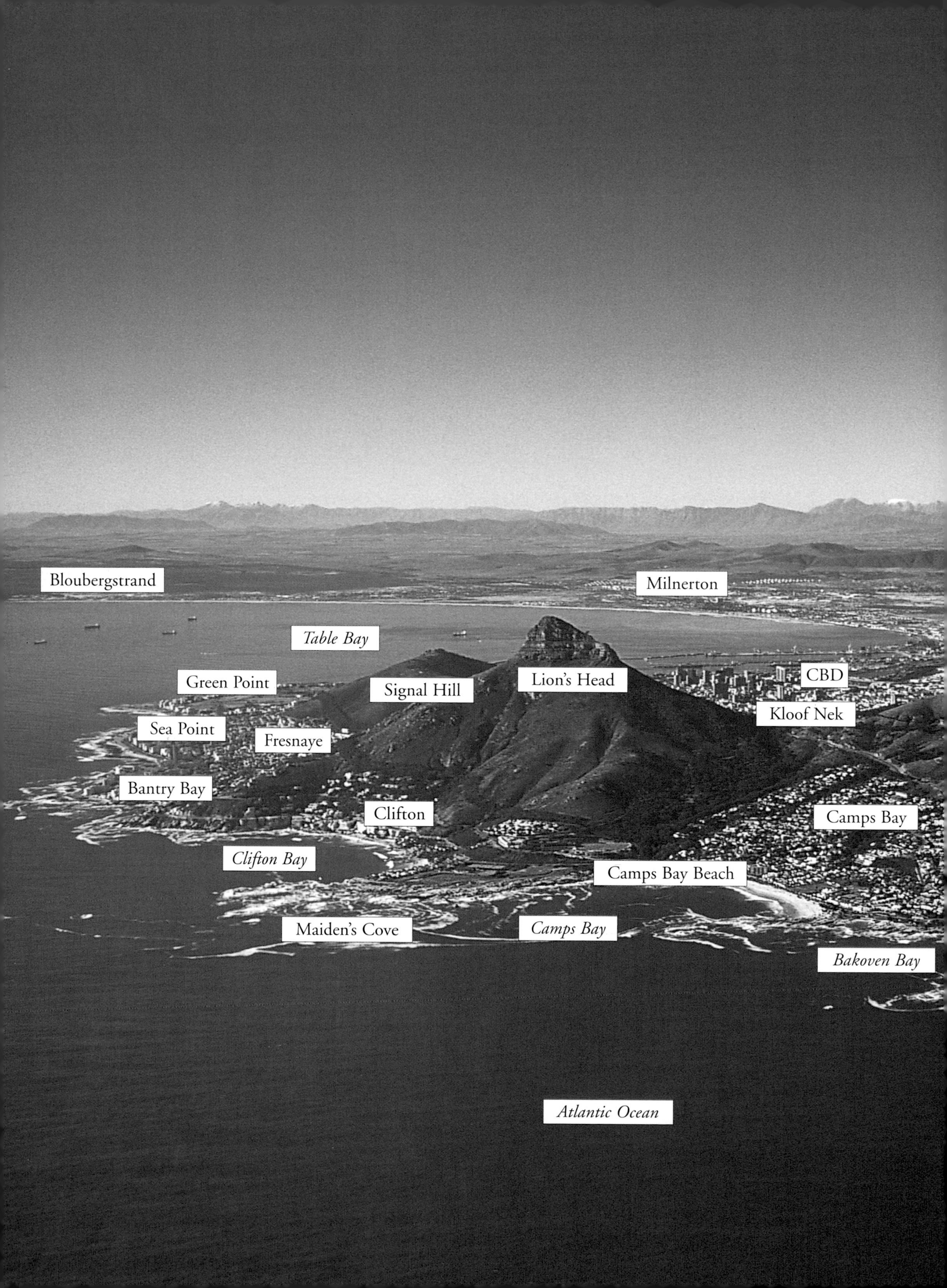

Bloubergstrand

Milnerton

Table Bay

Green Point

Signal Hill

Lion's Head

CBD

Kloof Nek

Sea Point

Fresnaye

Bantry Bay

Clifton

Camps Bay

Clifton Bay

Camps Bay Beach

Maiden's Cove

Camps Bay

Bakoven Bay

Atlantic Ocean

Table Mountain

Reservoirs

Twelve Apostles

Bakoven

Hout Bay ➡

acts which are making their way back to South Africa after many years of cultural isolation. International acts such as Paul Simon, Whitney Houston, U2, UB40, Roxette and Michael Jackson have all played under the night skies to an enthusiastic Cape Town audience jam-packed into the stadium. Sundays tend to be less noisy but just as frenetic, as bargain-hunters gather at the open-air market held each week in the stadium parking lot and surroundings. Shoppers can wander among a plethora of stalls offering handcrafted garments, household appliances, ethnic sculptures and costume jewellery.

Mouille Point

A tiny area to the west of the Victoria & Alfred Waterfront, and enclosed by the suburb of Green Point, **Mouille Point** is most noted for its wide vista of open ocean and conspicuous lighthouse. Erected by Herman Schutte as long ago as 1824, the **Mouille Point lighthouse**, with its haunting foghorn, is the oldest of its kind in the country. The light which once warned ships of the rocky coastline originally emanated from a simple oil lantern. This was not particularly reliable on misty Cape

evenings, but the modern device – of 850 000 candlepower – can be seen nearly 25 kilometres (15 miles) out to sea. Alongside the distinctive red-and-white striped structure is a small pleasure park for children, including a miniature golf course, train rides and an ice-cream stand. Virtually next door to the lighthouse is the **Serendipity Maze**, a tortuous series of hedged-in passageways that eventually lead to the centre, and a delight for small children.

Three Anchor Bay and Sea Point

On the seaward side of Signal Hill lies Three Anchor Bay and Sea Point, and the coastal stretch of Beach Road. The suburb of **Sea Point**, with its profusion of once-plush hotels and highrise accommodation, is one of the continent's most populated areas, and was once the playground of the rich and famous. Although property prices are still relatively high, Sea Point is no longer the sought-after residential area it once was. Nevertheless, it remains a hubbub of entertainment, boasting a lively strip of restaurants, all-night cafés and bistros, and trendy nightclubs. For an exciting alternative to the many Italian eateries and fast-food outlets, stop off at **New York Bagels**, the new self-service sit-down deli on the corner of Regent and Clarens roads. The concept is unique in South Africa: Upon entry, patrons are handed an electronic card, reserve their table of choice and then wander from one mouthwatering stall to the next, selecting from a varied menu that ranges from traditional Cape to Mediterranean – including several different kinds of bagels, of course. Once it's time to pay, the electronic card – which is 'swiped' through the system each time a selection is made at the food stations – is swiped through the till for the final total. Be sure to stop at the superb adjoining deli and bakery.

Sun-worshippers of all shapes and sizes tend to congregate along the three kilometres (two miles) of the **Sea Point Promenade**, popular among casual strollers, joggers and young rollerskaters and rollerbladers. The promenade, which includes a few small fast-food outlets and kiosks, looks out over popular **Rockland's Beach**. Offshore, the Atlantic Ocean is dotted with young surfers braving the notoriously icy waters. The area also boasts two safe seawater pools: **Saunder's Rock** and **Graaff's**

PREVIOUS PAGES *Cape Town's Atlantic coast embraces a clutch of plush residential enclaves, backed by the lofty Twelve Apostles.*

LEFT *Despite the warning provided by the historic Mouille Point lighthouse, many vessels have foundered on the rocky shore.*

OPPOSITE TOP *Blessed with breathtaking views, The Bay Hotel in Camps Bay is a haven of luxury.*

OPPOSITE BOTTOM *Camps Bay's long stretch of fine beach is the playground of bronzed volleyballers and sun-worshippers.*

Pool. Visitors should be aware that the latter is popular among male nudists. The recently revamped Sea Point Pavilion also has four enclosed seawater swimming pools, with the deepest boasting a 10-metre-high (30 feet) diving board.

The Leisure Strip

Southwest along the coast from Sea Point lies the band of upmarket residential properties unofficially known as **Millionaires' Mile**. Stretching along winding Victoria Road from Bantry Bay through Clifton, Camps Bay and Bakoven to distant Llandudno, this strip is considerably longer than a mile, but it is clearly the playground of the wealthy.

The wind-free, sun-blessed beaches provide an idyllic setting in which to relax – and the palatial homes along this coast are understandably expensive.

Beyond exclusive **Bantry Bay**, which nestles along the western slopes of Signal Hill and Lion's Head, lies sought-after **Clifton**, with its four immaculate beaches. Simply named First, Second, Third and Fourth, the Clifton beaches are famed the world over for their consummate splendour. The beaches are separated by granite outcrops which also act as a shelter from the southeasterly wind which plagues many of the Cape's less-favoured sunspots. Clifton is ideal for sunbathing and, in summer (December to February), the white sands are usually draped with scantily-clad bodies soaking up the Cape sun. First Beach is renowned for its sun-worshipping trendy set, while Third is a favourite of the teens, and Fourth Beach, with its nearby parking and refreshment facilities, caters mostly for family outings. The sun drenches these relatively secluded stretches virtually from sunrise to sunset, and revellers often party on into the night with picnic suppers and the occasional *braai* (barbecue). So, if you're prepared to fight it out with the

residents, hundreds of locals and other fun-seekers for the limited parking space, Clifton's beaches are the place to be if you want to experience the very best the Cape has to offer.

Luxury Living

Equally exclusive is **Camps Bay**, which lies at the foot of the Twelve Apostles – the mountain rampart that constitutes the western front of Table Mountain. Hedged in by granite boulders at each extreme, the enclave that is Camps Bay embraces a palm-fringed expanse of pristine white sand which looks as if it has come straight out of a Caribbean holiday brochure. Known in the late 1700s as Die Baay van Von Kamptz after Frederick von Kamptz, the owner of the original farm, Ravenstyn, Camps Bay is a lively, stylish place: Paragliders touch down dramatically on sands that play host to an exciting annual beach volleyball season, and holidaymakers picnic on the grassy margins, while children cavort in the tidal pools. There is even a bowling green for the less adventurous. But because Camps Bay is not as sheltered as Clifton, the wind can be an annoyance and the sea – although not suitable for surfing – can be volatile at times.

The landward side of Victoria Road is lined with shops, bistros – many with shaded pavement tables – and hotels. Overlooking the beach is the well-appointed **Bay Hotel**, boasting the sophisticated Rotunda ballroom. The Bay is a five-star affair, with prices to match its idyllic setting. One of the Cape's eternal favourites, **Blues** restaurant offers equally impressive vistas over Camps Bay beach. Having recently celebrated its tenth anniversary, it remains one of the city's finest dining experiences.

For a taste of the lively arts, take in one of the current shows at Camps Bay's intimate **Theatre on the Bay**, a local landmark which features scrolled drapery over its distinctive facade. After the theatre, enjoy dinner or sundowners at **Blues** or **Dizzy's Jazz Café**, with the famed Atlantic sunset at your feet.

Tucked away on Lion's Head above Camps Bay is the history-steeped **Round House** restaurant, originally built as a hunting lodge for Lord Charles Somerset, a 19th-century governor at the Cape. There is also **The Glen**, an ideal picnic area with excellent views. Legend has it that the spot is haunted by the tormented soul of Dr James Barry. If the day has proved too demanding, both Kloof Road – on which the Round House is located – and Camps Bay Drive will take weary travellers back over Lion's Head right into the City Bowl. But for the more energetic visitor, the remainder of the peninsula drive may prove to be the most exciting.

ABOVE *Carved mementoes and other crafts are offered for sale along the panoramic route between Bakoven and Llandudno.*

OPPOSITE *With many stretches of protected sand, Cape beaches are perfect for the young and the young at heart.*

Bakoven to Llandudno

Just beyond stylish Camps Bay is a small, rather isolated little beach seemingly hidden from the throng. Lying on Bakoven Bay, tiny **Bakoven beach** is not ideal for swimming or watersports – thick beds of seaweed and kelp clog the water – but is ideal for soaking up the sun. Unlike the more popular beaches, it does not cater for crowds so there are no shops or cafés. To reach this pebbly hideaway, you will have to brave the pathway down from the parking lot.

The road from Bakoven to Llandudno and beyond is a popular scenic drive. Just outside Bakoven, there is a substantial roadside market peppered with stalls selling curios such as seashells, carvings, biltong, and indigenous crafts. About halfway between Camps Bay and Llandudno lies a braai and picnic area with rockpools, and a string of tiny beaches popular with scuba divers who swim out to investigate the shipwreck just off the coast. The reserve at **Oudekraal** is also a popular recreational site. Recent proposals to develop this coastline have met opposition from Muslims – there are several holy sites in the area – and from environmentalists seeking to protect the fragile natural environment of the mountain slopes.

Despite the fact that the water of the Atlantic tends to be very cold, and swimming can be uncomfortable, the beaches along the Atlantic seaboard are perennially popular, and property prices are steep. Nowhere is this clearer than in the sought-after residential enclave of **Llandudno**, where luxury homes line the slopes that lead steeply down to a fine sandy beach. Once again, massive granite boulders shelter Llandudno's beach and residential area. The mood here is usually laid-back and slow, and perfect for relaxing on a hot day. The placid waters are deceptive, however, and have claimed their fair share of victims. The tanker *Romelia* came to grief off Sunset Rocks in 1977 while under tow, and the wreck may still be seen at low tide.

Further along is **Sandy Bay**, perhaps one of the Cape's most famous beaches and Cape Town's unofficial nudist hangout. Access is via Victoria and Llandudno roads. The latter winds

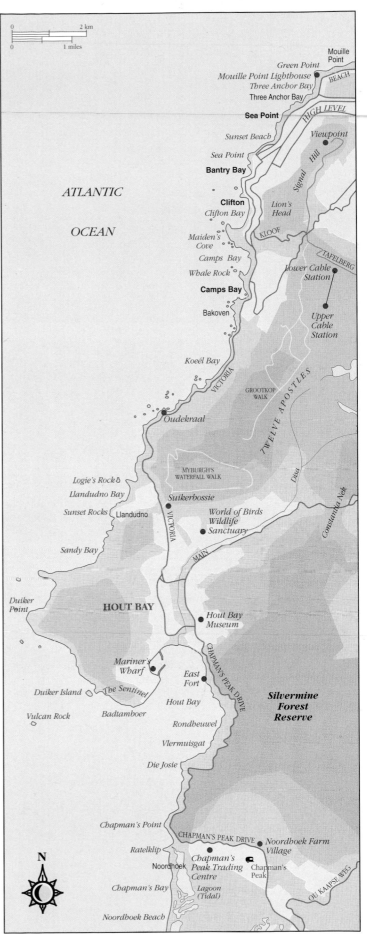

into Fishermen's Bend, and bathers should turn right into Oakburn Road and then left into Leeukoppie – the home of hotel magnate Sol Kerzner (of Sun City and Lost City fame) looks loftily from above – and into the carpark at Sunset Rocks. Because Sandy Bay is secluded, visitors will need to follow the footpath for about 15 to 20 minutes in order to reach the beach. The beach is surrounded by rocks and virtually impenetrable fynbos, making it ideal for bathing *au naturel*. Sadly, the natural splendour of Sandy Bay is also threatened by development, but bathers may still enjoy a day under the African sun.

Perched on the slopes of Klein Leeukoppie, just a few kilometres from Llandudno along Victoria Road, is **Suikerbossie**. This celebrated tearoom and restaurant serves an outstanding menu, and kosher meals are also readily available. This delightful stopover is an immensely popular venue for both afternoon tea and lunch – in fact, be sure to book for a Sunday – and offers magnificent views across the waters of Hout Bay.

Hout Bay

Because of its relative seclusion and the staunch 'patriotism' of its 'citizens', the fishing village of **Hout Bay** has unofficially become known as the Republic of Hout Bay, and realistic passports may even be purchased from enthusiastic custodians. Visitors may reach Hout Bay either from Victoria Road and Suikerbossie, or from the southern suburbs via Constantia Nek. From the city centre, buses depart quite regularly before 9:00am, at noon, and again between 14:15 and 17:30 from the OK Bazaars in Adderley Street.

Despite rapid expansion in recent years, the fishing village that is Hout Bay remains relatively unscathed by modern development, and maintains a decidedly rural atmosphere. As a centre for many home-based industries, artists and craft traders, the village remains true to its harbour origins. Its name comes from the Dutch (and Afrikaans) word for timber, for the valley was a source of wood during the early days of the Cape colony. Hout Bay is still an important fishing harbour, and is renowned throughout the country for its fresh fish and seafood – be sure to make a stop at **Snoekies**, the city's favourite fresh fish market. Crayfish and other seafood delicacies are exported directly from the docks, and the **Snoek Festival** is held in June and July. Throughout the year, and especially during the annual **Hout Bay Festival** in August, enthusiastic crowds flock to the harbour, crowded

with boats of every description, and to the **Mariner's Wharf** complex, with its outstanding seafood restaurant, fish markets and curio shops. An exciting alternative to the standard shopping experience is to buy an oyster – guaranteed to contain a pearl – from the **Pearl Factory**, and open it to find out whether your investment paid off in the form of a perfect pearl.

Pleasure seekers will find that Hout Bay offers many diversions: the long, curving beach provides safe and enjoyable swimming; small sailboats are available for hire; and there are a number of cruise operators in the area. **Circe Launches** offers sundowner cruises to the V&A Waterfront, Duiker Island (seabirds and seals) and Seal Island, while **Game Fish Charters** offers deep-sea game-fishing.

The character and ambience of the village of Hout Bay is at its best during the regular pavement flea market. Hout Bay's Main Road is much like that of any small hamlet, with a spattering of craft and clothing shops, banking and commercial activity, and steakhouses and other eateries. One of the most remarkable buildings, however, is **Kronendal**. This Cape Dutch home was built at the turn of the 18th century by Johannes van Helsdingen and is Cape Town's only surviving example of the typical H-plan of the period. Having been both a tearoom and an antique dealership, Kronendal is once again a restaurant. **Cranzgot's**, on Harbour Road, is a live music venue, throbbing with the sounds of many top local artists. Also on Harbour Road is **The Big Blue** (formerly Dirty Dick's), a relaxed and convivial watering hole popular with locals and visitors.

For a peek into the absorbing history of Hout Bay and to enquire about one of the many walks

OPPOSITE TOP *Hardworking fisherfolk offer their fresh fare at Hout Bay's old harbour.*

OPPOSITE MIDDLE *Hout Bay is a haven for the peninsula's many craftspeople – and for curio-buying visitors.*

OPPOSITE BOTTOM *With the atmosphere of a fishing village, Mariner's Wharf is an emporium of seaside delights.*

ABOVE *From across Hout Bay, the bold silhouette of The Sentinel marks the entrance to the bay.*

RIGHT *Competing with over 400 species at the World of Birds, the scarlet ibis boasts perhaps the most arresting plumage.*

69

residents include the colourful, chattering macaws, majestic blue cranes, penguins and a collection of formidable-looking owls.

Chapman's Peak Drive

At the start of the Cape's most spectacular and most scenic drive stands the **Chapman's Peak Hotel**. Its expansive, shaded verandah is a popular eatery in the summer months – the cosy interior is ideal in winter – and serves some of the finest seafood available on the peninsula. Visitors may also notice the bronze statue of a leopard atop the rocks close to the shore. This statue commemorates the Cape leopard, the last surviving of which was killed in Hout Bay, an area once teeming with wildlife.

Nail-biting **Chapman's Peak Drive** – excavated from the mountainface at the boundary between the soft sandstone and hard granite layers and opened in 1922 – winds precariously for approximately 10 kilometres (6 miles) from Hout Bay to Noordhoek. The winding route represents the most visually spectacular – as well as the most physically demanding – segment of both The Cape Argus–Pick 'n Pay Cycle Tour (March) and the Two Oceans Marathon (April). The peak itself is about 600 metres (1 970 feet) high and, naturally, affords unsurpassed views over the ocean below. The multitude of roadside vantage points allows visitors the

and trails among the unspoilt terrain of the area, visit the **Hout Bay Museum** on St Andrews Road. For those who want to know more about natural history, a visit to the **World of Birds** on Valley Road really is a must. Initiated by well-known local resident Walter Mangold as a rescue station for sick or wounded birds, World of Birds is home to more than 450 indigenous species housed in spacious aviaries. Bird enthusiasts and casual visitors can walk through the carefully designed habitats within the cages. Highlights among the facility's more than 3 000

Chapman's Bay Trading Post, a cluster of craft and clothing shops that also houses a coffee bar and the popular **Red Herring** restaurant and pub within its milkwood-shaded precincts. Further along the main road toward Fish Hoek and Kommetjie lies **Noordhoek Farm Village**, a charming collection of whitewashed buildings that shelter craft outlets, a farmstall and a popular restaurant and pub.

This rather rustic corner of the peninsula is one of the most treasured examples of Cape Town's natural heritage. To truly appreciate the splendour of the Atlantic seaboard, it is recommended that visitors take a leisurely drive back toward the city via Noordhoek and Hout Bay along Chapman's Peak Drive as the sun sets. The experience is quite unforgettable.

opportunity to take in one of the peninsula's most magnificent sights, and the sunsets here are particularly breathtaking. The road is narrow, so motorists should always exercise caution on this route. To the north, the sheer cliffs of The Sentinel loom over the entrance to Hout Bay. To the south lies Noordhoek and the scenic route to Cape Point.

Noordhoek

Most renowned for its pristine beach and unsullied environment, **Noordhoek** has become the favoured playground of Capetonians who wish to escape the frenzy of city life in favour of the rural tranquillity of farms and smallholdings. Many artists live here, and the Noordhoek Art Route provides much to tempt art-lovers. From October to May, on the first Sunday of the month, the art route's dozen or so artists open their studios to the public. However, individual studios can also be visited at other times by arrangement with the artist.

Sparkling Noordhoek Beach, on the west end of Noordhoek Valley, covers about eight kilometres (5 miles) of coastline from the foot of Chapman's Peak to the fishing village of Kommetjie. Although it is well suited to sunbathing or a leisurely seaside stroll, the waters here are quite dangerous.

The **Chapman's Bay Trading Centre** at the corner of Beach Road and Pine Street in Noordhoek is a unique craft centre which goes about its fascinating day-to-day operations as the public wanders through the workshop. The centre forms part of

OPPOSITE TOP *From the comfort of a tour boat, visitors come face to face with Seal Island's famed inhabitants.*

OPPOSITE BOTTOM *The awe-inspiring scenic drive around Chapman's Peak is surpassed only by its superlative sunsets.*

ABOVE *The long, white beach at Noordhoek offers plenty of room for horseback riding, as well as other pursuits.*

False Bay

Day Five

FALSE BAY

Muizenberg · St James · Kalk Bay · Fish Hoek · Simon's Town · Miller's Point · Smitswinkelbaai
Cape of Good Hope Nature Reserve · Scarborough · Kommetjie · Imhoff's Gift · Silvermine Nature Reserve

The natural bay that stretches along the peninsula's eastern coastline from the Cape of Good Hope Nature Reserve at Cape Point to Cape Hangklip came to be known as False Bay because early navigators mistook Hangklip for Cape Point. The error resulted in many shipwrecks along this hazardous shoreline, but today the shores of False Bay are lined with small coastal towns, and the land varies from compact suburbia to long stretches of natural beach. Access to the area from the centre of Cape Town is via the Blue Route (M3), or along Prince George's Drive, which extends as far as Muizenberg. The scenic mountain road via Boyes Drive, in turn, commands impressive views over the seaside suburbs of Muizenberg and St James. Visitors can follow the beautiful coastal route through Lakeside, Muizenberg, St James, Kalk Bay, Fish Hoek, and Simon's Town to Cape Point. Each route has its drawcards, but the most exciting must surely be the sight of the southern right whales which congregate between May and September in order to calve in the waters of False Bay.

Within the bay itself lies **Seal Island**, a breeding ground for both the Cape fur seal and many species of seabirds, and – because of the plentiful prey – the hunting ground of the great white shark. Although it is always advisable to be on the lookout for these much-feared – and often-seen – predators, few attacks have been reported in recent years, and even fewer have proven disastrous for bathers. For those who may want to take a closer look at these great, white hunters of the seas, contact Adventure Safaris & Sport Tours, Southcoast Seafaris or White Shark Ecoventures based in the city.

Muizenberg

Nestled against the slopes of Muizenberg Mountain, 25 kilometres from the city, the town of **Muizenberg** has its origins in the very early days of the Cape when the coastal strip was first settled by Europeans. The Battle of Muizenberg was fought here in 1795 between the British and the Dutch. In the early years of the 20th century, Muizenberg became one of the

PREVIOUS PAGES *Jutting fingerlike into the Atlantic is the appropriately named Cape Point, centrepiece of the scenic Cape of Good Hope Nature Reserve.*

INSET *The sometimes insolent antics of troops of resident chacma baboons delight visitors to Cape Point.*

ABOVE *The colony of jackass penguins which take refuge at Boulders Beach near Simon's Town are protected by law.*

OPPOSITE *Reminiscent of the 1920s, when the small seaside town was a popular resort, brightly painted bathing boxes line the small beach at St James.*

country's most favoured holiday resorts, and a string of impressive homes was erected on the mountainside overlooking False Bay. Soon, however, many of the old Edwardian and Victorian homes were joined by representatives of more recent architectural styles. As a result, the modern township is a charming mix of the old villas, fishermen's cottages, and colonial structures – such as the fine red-brick Edwardian building on Muizenberg Station, with its grand spiral staircase (and now housing both a shop and restaurant) – and the modern elements, which include the 29-storey Cinnabar building and the Muizenberg Promenade and Pavilion.

The Sandvlei lagoon area which today seems to form the centre of the built-up area was originally established as a cattle post. Today the banks of the lagoon are lined with a small bird sanctuary to the north – and a variety of housing complexes. The most noticeable is the **Marina da Gama** development to the east. Sandvlei is fed by the salt water of the Atlantic, and the lagoon has become the domain of both waterfowl and watersport enthusiasts. Windsurfers and canoeists ply the waters of the lagoon and the sea off Muizenberg.

Surfing and angling are undoubtedly among the principal reasons for Muizenberg's popularity. Muizenberg Beach and Sunrise Beach – the white sands to the northeast which cater largely for residents of the Cape Flats – boast most modern facilities, including change rooms, public toilets, parking and a multitude of amusements such as camel rides, fast-food outlets, miniature golf and train and boat rides for children.

The striped roof of **Muizenberg Pavilion** may be seen from afar. The pavilion usually resounds with the laughter of children splashing in the saltwater pool or cavorting down the popular water slide. The parking lot and paved area below the pavilion also hosts a Sunday-morning flea market whenever the weather permits. The pinnacled centre itself is often rented out for public functions, and its main source of interest is its refreshment stands, fast-food kiosk and Indian restaurant. However, a wooden walkway – leading all the way over the rocks to St James in the west, and popular among afternoon strollers – and a promenade leading off to the east certainly make up for any lack of excitement. The modern concrete promenade replaced the original structure built in the early 1900s, and offers a splendid view over the ocean and the wave-lapped beaches – usually packed with bathers stretched out among the vibrant bathing huts erected on the beach in the late 19th century and recently renovated. From the promenade spring visitors can also spot the whales gambolling in False Bay.

If the children tire of frolicking in the water, the **Toy Museum and Collectors' Shop** in the Sir Herbert Baker-designed manor house at No. 8 Beach Road will certainly get their attention. The museum is dedicated to the craft of toy manufacture, and will prove a delight for starry-eyed little ones.

Displays include model trains, cars and aeroplanes, and, of course, the much-loved Victorian rocking horse, porcelain dolls and teddy bears.

The small whitewashed cottage known as **Het Post Huijs** on Main Road was built in 1673, and is the oldest inhabitable European house in the country, predating even the Castle of Good Hope. It was originally used as a signal station, house and fort under the auspices of the Dutch East India Company (VOC), and today it houses an exhibition devoted to the story of the Battle of Muizenberg.

The drive between Muizenberg and St James is lined with stately mansions, but at least two stand out. The Italian-style building at number 192 Main Road was once the home of Count Natale Labia. Now known as the **Natale Labia Museum** and a satellite branch of the South African National Gallery, it houses works of art collected by the Italian nobleman before his death in 1936. The museum has its own tearoom, **Café Labia**, and hosts lectures, exhibitions and musical performances.

ABOVE *Muizenberg's famed stretch of beach is a popular drawcard for surfers who flock to ride the impressive waves of False Bay.*

BELOW *From the fishing village of Kommetjie, in the foreground, fynbos-clad mountains stretch toward Cape Point.*

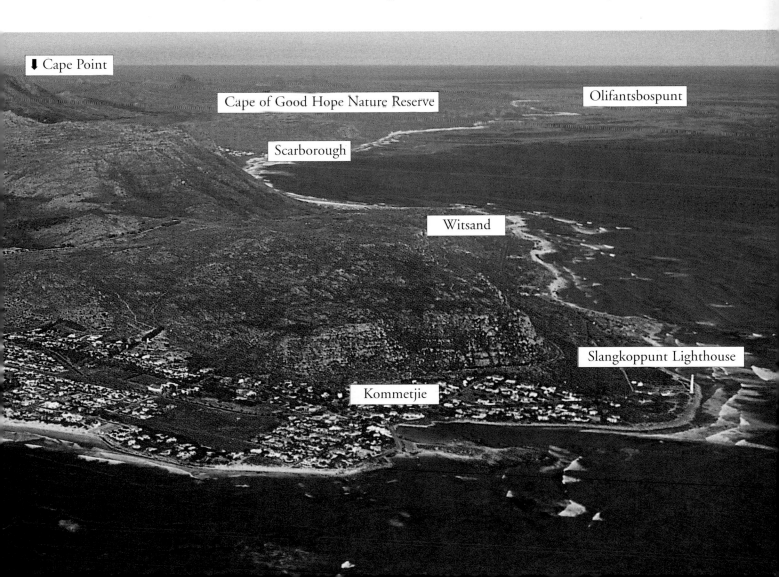

Cape Point

Cape of Good Hope Nature Reserve

Olifantsbospunt

Scarborough

Witsand

Slangkoppunt Lighthouse

Kommetjie

Further along Main Road is the equally impressive **Rust-en-Vrede**, the home of mining tycoon Sir Abe Bailey and designed by Sir Herbert Baker. It remains a private home so is not open for viewing, but certainly worth a visit is the little stone bungalow at No. 246, which stands out among the many imposing houses stretching down the mountainside. This is the **Rhodes Cottage Museum**, the holiday home of Cape premier and tycoon Cecil John Rhodes. The simple house displays items of Rhodes's personal memorabilia.

St James

Legend has it that the first parish priest stationed at the St James Catholic Church, erected in 1854, refused to accept his post unless a railway station was erected to encourage parishioners to attend mass. Needless to say, the railway station and the suburb that grew up around it all became known as **St James**, and the church still serves Catholic worshippers from near and far.

Largely because of limited building space on the mountain slopes and narrow verges, St James has seen relatively little development. Situated as it is at the foot of Kalk Bay Mountain (Kalkbaaiberg), St James and its surroundings remain immensely attractive. The natural beauty encompasses not only Kalkbaaiberg – the mountain's original Dutch name – but also a number of natural features such as rock pools, small waterfalls, streams and caves such as Tartarus, Erica and Jubilee, making it ideal for casual walks, hikes and bird-watching. The plotted walk through the Spes Bona Valley Forest starts at Boyes Drive above St James and takes hikers past splendid wild olive trees, indigenous yellowwoods and the

ABOVE *The coast at Muizenberg has long been a haunt of local fishermen who ply the waters of False Bay.*

RIGHT *A humble thatched cottage on Main Road, Muizenberg, was the holiday cottage of the ailing tycoon, Cecil John Rhodes.*

rooi els (red elder) for which the area has become so well known, and ends at Tartarus Cave.

The small, sheltered stretch of sand on the seaward side of Main Road below, is dotted with brightly coloured bathing boxes much like those at Muizenberg, and is popular with children. It has a multitude of tiny rock pools and, of course, a walled tidal pool. Divers and surfers congregate at Danger Beach, a little further south.

Kalk Bay

A surfing mecca with a decidedly bohemian atmosphere, the fishing village of **Kalk Bay** was first inhabited by Europeans in the 1600s when shipwrecked sailors took refuge in the many caves that dot the mountainside. The bay is named for the kilns built by the VOC in which seashells were burned to make lime for building cement – 'kalk' is the Dutch word for lime. In the early 19th century, the protected bay below Trappiekop on Kalkbaaiberg became an active harbour catering largely for the fishermen and whalers who worked the southern coast. The slopes of the mountain are still dotted with the humble homes of the descendants of these fisherfolk, but little remains of the once thriving industry. Still, a small fleet of brightly painted fishing vessels continues to ply the southern waters for snoek and other fish, especially during June and July.

The fishermen return to Kalk Bay with their catch around noon. The fish is always straight out of the water, and definitely worth the price. If you aren't prepared to gut and descale the fish yourself, the fishermen will do it for you. Visitors can even take a trip out with the fishermen (contact the harbour master), but an easier way to sample the local dishes is to visit the nearby **Brass Bell** restaurant. Because this restaurant and pub are situated on Kalk Bay railway station, visitors may want to take

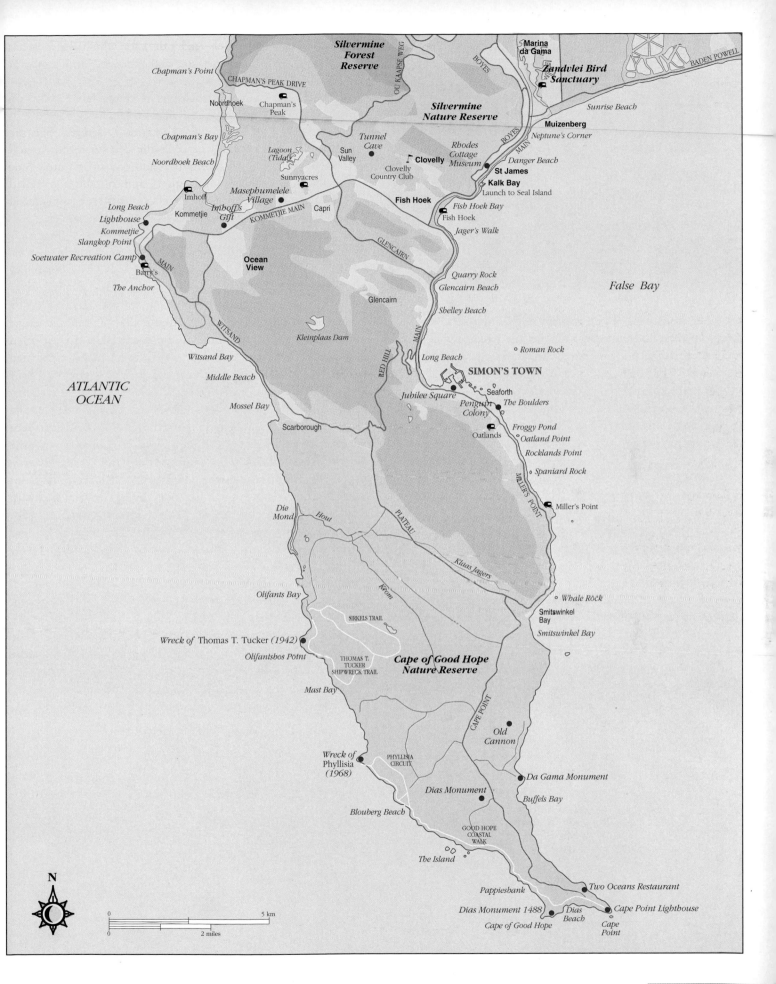

Silvermine
Forest
Reserve

Chapman's Point

CHAPMAN'S PEAK DRIVE

Noordhoek

Chapman's
Peak

Chapman's Bay

Noordhoek Beach

Lagoon
(Tidal)

Sun
Valley

Tunnel
Cave

Silvermine
Nature Reserve

Rhodes
Cottage
Museum

Sunnyacres

Masephumelele
Village

Imhoff

Kommetjie

Imhoff's
Gift

KOMMETJIE MAIN

Capri

Clovelly

Clovelly
Country Club

St James

Danger Beach

Kalk Bay

Launch to Seal Island

Long Beach

Lighthouse

Kommetjie

Slangkop Point

Soetwater Recreation Camp

Barry's

The Anchor

Ocean
View

Fish Hoek

Fish Hoek Bay

Fish Hoek

Jager's Walk

GLENCAIRN

Quarry Rock

Glencairn Beach

Glencairn

Shelley Beach

False Bay

WITSAND

MAIN

Witsand Bay

Middle Beach

Mossel Bay

Scarborough

Kleinplaas Dam

RED HILL

MAIN

Long Beach

Roman Rock

SIMON'S TOWN

ATLANTIC
OCEAN

Jubilee Square

Seaforth

Penguin
Colony

The Boulders

Froggy Pond

Oatlands

Oatland Point

Rocklands Point

Spaniard Rock

MILLER'S POINT

Miller's Point

Die
Mond

Hout

PLATEAU

Krom

Klaas Jagers

Olifants Bay

SIRKELS TRAIL

Whale Rock

Smitswinkel
Bay

Smitswinkel Bay

Wreck of Thomas T. Tucker (1942)

Olifantsbos Point

THOMAS T.
TUCKER
SHIPWRECK TRAIL

Cape of Good Hope
Nature Reserve

Mast Bay

CAPE POINT

Old
Cannon

Wreck of
Phyllisia
(1968)

PHYLLISIA
CIRCUIT

Dias Monument

Da Gama Monument

Buffels Bay

Blouberg Beach

GOOD HOPE
COASTAL
WALK

The Island

Pappiesbank

Two Oceans Restaurant

Dias Monument 1488

Dias
Beach

Cape Point Lighthouse

Cape of Good Hope

Cape
Point

N

0   5 km

0   2 miles

Marina
da Gama

Zandvlei Bird
Sanctuary

BOYES

BADEN POWELL

OU KAAPSE WEG

Sunrise Beach

Muizenberg

Neptune's Corner

BOYES

MAIN

the train from Cape Town central station. Just a few metres away from the harbour, the Brass Bell has become well known for its superb menu, and especially for its seafood. The restaurant is ideally situated right on the water's edge, and is extremely popular during the summer holiday season when there is barely enough room to move in either the restaurant or the bar. Live music is a regular feature, as are the fish *braais*, and the sandy beach and tidal pools below are particularly popular with local families.

The main coastal road which runs through Kalk Bay is lined with quaint shops and cafés, each specialising in something different: ceramics, paintings, driftwood art, bric-à-brac, antiques (both genuine and not quite authentic) and other remnants of a bygone era.

Fish Hoek

The little hamlet of **Fish Hoek** was established in 1918, but has grown considerably in recent years. **Fish Hoek** is most noted for its long, gentle beach and for whale viewing in late winter and early spring. The beach is popular with horse-riders, while kite-fliers converge on the sands on the frequent windy days. It is safe to swim along this picturesque strip – set aside as a marine reserve, like the rest of the False Bay coast – and the warm waters are suited to both surfing and sailing. Anglers congregate on the rocks nearby or try their luck from small boats further out in the bay. Among the facilities are changing rooms,

ablution facilities and even a playground and restaurant. Life in this town is decidedly laid-back and relaxing; a popular pastime is a stroll along **Jager's Walk**, a concrete catwalk which stretches along the rocky shoreline from Fish Hoek towards Simon's Town, offering panoramic views of the Bay.

The **False Bay Fire Museum** on Brakloof Road is a collection of old and new firefighting equipment and machinery, including yellowing photographs and age-old uniforms. Tours and visits are by appointment only.

The mountain slopes behind Fish Hoek reach as far as Noordhoek Valley. In **Peers Cave** – follow the signs from 20th Avenue – a number of ancient burial sites were discovered by Victor Peers in 1927. Surrounded by San rock paintings on the cave walls, the oldest specimen is at least 12 000 years old and the ancient remains have since become known as Fish Hoek Man. The primitive stone implements found here may still be viewed at the **Fish Hoek Valley Museum** on Central Circle, and the museum also arranges organised hiking trails.

Beyond Fish Hoek lies the picturesque village of **Simon's Town**, home base of the South African Navy. For those who don't wish to see the town or would prefer to take a shorter route directly to Scarborough rather than the coastal route to Cape Point, the turnoff over Red Hill is an ideal shortcut. It is, however, worth driving through Simon's Town. Small taxis called 'Rikkis' also ferry visitors to the gates of the Cape of Good Hope Nature Reserve. Just beyond the turnoff to the grave of Able Seaman Just Nuisance outside the South African Naval Signal School is the road up Simonsberg, which provides an excellent vantage point from which to view the bay below. The road leads right into the little village of Scarborough on the Atlantic seaboard. Visitors should be aware that, for security reasons, you are not allowed to photograph the naval base.

En route to Simon's Town

Just before you reach Simon's Town – on Dido Valley Road off Red Hill Road – lies the world's biggest polished gemstone factory. At **Topstones**, polishing and tumbling machines turn rough rocks into semi-precious stones. The plant is open to the public and is very popular with children who scramble through

---

TOP *Fishermen like this one set out each day from the fishing village of Kalk Bay. The arrival of the catch is a daily highlight.*

LEFT *The Boulders, near Simon's Town, offers the endearing sight of a mother jackass penguin fussing over one of her chicks.*

OPPOSITE TOP *The long, gentle, sun-drenched beach at Fish Hoek draws plenty of watersport enthusiasts and bathers.*

OPPOSITE BOTTOM *A port since the earliest days of European settlement, Simon's Town is the base of the South African Navy.*

the mounds of polished and unpolished stones searching for the perfect gem. Purchase a bucket upon entry, and you are allowed to take home all that the container can hold.

From here the road to Simon's Town has a clear view over the bay and is a favourite spot for whale watching during the calving season. Also dotted along this rugged coastline are traces of the many ships which have come to grief on the rocky shores over the centuries, among them the SS *Clan Stuart*, *Bato*, *Die Gebroeders*, *Katwyk Aan Rhyn*, *Parama* and the *Phoenix* on the other side of Selbourne Dry Dock. The expanse of white sand – aptly named Long Beach – which stretches along this route has long been the playground of the inhabitants of Simon's Town. Long Beach ends at the station – the last stop on the Southern Suburbs railway line – at the entrance to the town.

Early Simon's Town

The historic town traces its origins to Simon van der Stel who, as governor of the relatively new settlement, decided that the bay was an ideal harbour for the Dutch fleet during the winter months. It was, however, only after Baron von Imhoff set up a proper port and dockland here in 1743 that Simon's Bay began to take on the naval responsibilities it enjoys today. For nearly 150 years, the town was the South Atlantic base for the Royal Navy, and only came under South African control in 1957. The naval influence is still very much in evidence. Uniformed naval

personnel stroll the same cobbled pavements as sailors of old, and many of the townsfolk are either employed by the navy or the adjoining dockyard.

Simon's Town, however, is not only a bastion of the military, but provides a delightful look into the history of the country. Although the main road running through the village changes its name at regular intervals – Main Road, it becomes Station Road, St George's Street, Queens Road, Macfarlane Road and back to Main – it is indeed a single road, and one crammed

with memories of yesteryear. The Simon's Town Publicity Association offers a 1.2-kilometre (3/4 mile) guided walk along a historic route starting at the railway station and ending at the East Dockyard, and the Flora Conservation Group arranges walks in the fynbos on Simonsberg.

Many of the oldest parts of the town and especially the working dockyard date back to the early days of the Cape. The Lower North Battery was built by the Dutch over 200 years ago, and today serves as the Gunnery School's firing range, while the West Dockyard was the site of the first store and naval hospital selected by Baron von Imhoff.

Simon's Town Today

The first place of interest on entering the town – and certainly one of its most famous – is elegant **Admiralty House** off Station Road, historically the home of the naval commander and now open to the public. The gabled manor was built in typical Cape Regency style by VOC official Antoni Vissir in the early 19th century and served as the Cape residence of visiting naval officials, ships' captains, royalty and other distinguished travellers – for whom the upper storey was added – until it was sold to the Royal Navy.

Perhaps one of the most charming old buildings in Simon's Town's is the **Church of St Francis** on Court Road, which dates back to 1837. According to local legend, the little church may be the oldest Anglican church in the country, and was consecrated five years after its construction by the visiting Bishop of Tasmania. Originally named after Lady Frances Cole, who helped raise the money required to build the church, the name has since been changed to commemorate Francis of Assisi, the patron saint of animals.

Court Road is also home to **The Residency**, which now houses the Simon's Town Museum and tourism and information office. Over the years, the building has served as the offices of the magistrate, the governor's retreat, hospital, slave quarters and prison – see the cells and the stocks in which prisoners were confined – but today it tells the story of the town and particularly its naval connection.

Jubilee Square is the heart of Simon's Town, and its busy arcade of shops, market stalls and cafés looks down over the harbour. It is on this public square that the bronze statue of Able Seaman Just Nuisance commemorates one of the town's most famous residents. Many ships have mascots but none achieved such fame as that of HMS *Neptune* and HMS *Afrikander I*, the Great Dane who 'enlisted' in the Royal Navy in 1939. The dog was so loved by his comrades-in-arms during the war that, on his death in 1943, Just Nuisance, wrapped in the White Ensign, was buried with full naval honours.

To the north of Jubilee Square is the **False Bay Yacht Club** – offering yachts and fishing boats for charter – and, to the right, the old **Stempastorie**. This was originally the home of the resident Dutch Reformed minister and where, in 1919, the

Reverend Marthinus de Villiers wrote the score for *Die Stem*, once the national anthem of South Africa and now joint anthem with *Nkosi Sikeleli Africa* (God Bless Africa). The Stempastorie museum also displays the history of South Africa's flags, national emblems and coats of arms.

The **Warrior Toy Museum** on St George's Street will undoubtedly be popular with the little ones, as it boasts a wide collection of both antique and more recent children's toys, including old dolls, trains and original lead soldiers dating back to the 1700s.

Roman Rock Lighthouse at the harbour entrance was erected in 1861 to guide the increasing number of ships visiting Simon's Town into the precarious bay. Still in working order, it is said to be the third oldest lighthouse in South Africa, and the only one to be purposely built on a rock.

In the shadow of the Roman Rock Lighthouse lies the West Dockyard and in it the **Martello Tower** and **Naval Museum**. The exhibits here cover naval ships, South Africa's maritime history and the story of the men and women who served in the country's fleet. There is also an authentic recreation of a pub as it would have looked during the Second World War, and displays of mementoes left by Lord Nelson, hero of the Battle of Trafalgar in 1805.

Nearing the southern limit of Simon's Town is popular **Seaforth Beach**, one of the last on this route to cater for the needs of families. Bathing in the crystal waters of this protected beach is quite safe, and there are lawns for picnicking, a parking area and a waterslide.

The coastline beyond Simon's Town has little to offer either the historian or the casual sightseer but its natural beauty is considered by many to be unsurpassed on the peninsula. The flora and fauna here has been virtually untouched by mankind, and much of it is protected by law. Just outside Simon's Town is the secluded enclave of **Boulders Beach**, known also as The Boulders, or simply Boulders. The beach is home to a colony of endangered jackass penguins, and is protected by the massive rounded granite outcrops from which it gets its name. The waters of this sheltered beach are both warm and safe. There is a small entrance fee to the penguin rookery. One of the few human intrusions permitted along this coast is the Simon's Town Country Club and golf course, situated about a third of the way between Simon's Town and Miller's Point.

OPPOSITE *Many of the charming arcaded buildings lining Simon's Town's Main Road date back to the 19th century.*

TOP *In a city renowned for its seafood, one of the finest seafood menus is offered by the Black Marlin, near Miller's Point.*

RIGHT *The only canine to enlist in the Royal Navy, Able Seaman Just Nuisance is commemorated with a statue on Jubilee Square.*

Miller's Point and Smitswinkelbaai

Beyond Froggy Farm and Murdock Valley, with its well-known and appropriately named Fishermen's Beach, lies beautiful **Miller's Point**. The area buzzes with activity in spring, when southern right, humpback and Bryde's whales congregate at the point. There is a caravan park – generally booked up in the holiday season – and a tidal pool, and it is here too that crayfish divers and snorkellers converge to either harvest the plentiful crustaceans or explore the marine life. Miller's Point is also the home of the **Black Marlin**, one of the country's most highly acclaimed seafood restaurants.

Just off the point where the road turns back into the Cape of Good Hope Nature Reserve lies tranquil **Smitswinkelbaai**, a cosy enclave of private cottages inaccessible by road. The waters of this bay are ideal for both swimming and fishing, but there is a steep path leading to the beach.

The short distance between Smitswinkelbaai and the gates to the Cape of Good Hope Nature Reserve has its own attractions. The winding road ascends, providing spectacular views of the precipitous coastline and the waters of False Bay. Just outside the entrance to the reserve, visitors will find an open-air roadside market crammed with carved animals, African masks and wooden statuettes – most produced in Zimbabwe. Just 500 metres (1 525 feet) beyond the reserve gates is the Cape Point Ostrich Farm. Although primarily a working farm – there is no ostrich riding or racing offered – visitors are welcome to wander through this former chicken farm, which has been renovated to cater for the breeding of these strange-looking flightless birds. Tours include the incubators, hatchery and rearing pens. Naturally, choice cuts of ostrich meat figure on the menu at the farm restaurant, and leather and feather products are available at the shop.

The Cape of Good Hope Nature Reserve

Encompassing the entire southern tip of the peninsula and Cape Point, the **Cape of Good Hope Nature Reserve** is a protected paradise only an hour's drive from the city centre and is visited by more than 400 000 people every year. The 40 kilometres (25 miles) of the reserve's coastline extends from Smitswinkelbaai on False Bay through Buffelsbaai, Cape Point, Mast Bay, Olifantsbospunt and Schuster Bay to Scarborough on the Atlantic seaboard. Entrance to the reserve is limited to a single road and the conservation of the ecosystem is a high priority for the custodians. Although picnic and braai facilities have been specially designated for public use and there are a number of signposted walking routes and places of interest, all the normal rules pertaining to protected areas apply. Visitors to the marine reserve are permitted to leave their car — except, of course, in the restricted areas — but are warned that officials do not take kindly to the damage that is done either to the natural environment or the animals that are found there, nor to unlawful fishing and crayfishing within its waters.

The baboons often encountered along the roadside have become so accustomed to handouts from curious onlookers that their natural instinct to hunt has been replaced by the need to scavenge. As a result, they can be very aggressive in their determination to feed, and have been known to attack. Visitors are warned not to open car windows or to offer the baboons food. All visitors are advised to pick up a copy of the visitors' rules available at the information kiosk at the reserve entrance.

The reserve's nearly 8 000-hectare (19 768 acres) area is home to over a thousand different floral species and an extraordinary wealth of wildlife, including birds, reptiles, fish and large and small mammals. Among the smaller species to be found here are the dassie, Cape fox, and baboon. Larger mammals include Cape mountain zebra and a variety of antelope species, such as the endangered bontebok — which is endemic to the southwestern Cape — and eland. The waters are inhabited by migrating whales, dolphins and seals.

Top Right *The scenic wonder of Cape Point draws large numbers of tourists to its awe-inspiring views of the Atlantic Ocean.*

Middle Right *The Cape of Good Hope Nature Reserve provides a protected haven for animals such as the Cape bontebok.*

Bottom Right *Cape Point's Two Oceans Restaurant offers diners panoramic views of False Bay's majestic coastline.*

Opposite Top *The old lighthouse at Cape Point is today a prime vantage point.*

Opposite Bottom *A funicular railway offers visitors a less taxing route up to the lookout at Cape Point.*

The halfway mark between Smitswinkelbaai and Cape Point is picturesque **Buffelsbaai**, the starting point for some splendid walks among the fynbos and rocky landscape. Buffelsbaai has its own slipway for fishing boats, as well as picnicking and swimming areas and a tidal pool. There is a shipwreck just off the coast, and angling is permitted from the beach.

On the rocky shore stands a monument to Vasco da Gama. Just inland is the stone cross erected in memory of Bartolomeu Dias, the first European explorer to view — but not land on — this remote area of the southern Cape. Dias first named the peninsula the Cape of Storms, but then changed it to the Cape of Good Hope as he neared the end of his journey, which he hoped would lead him to the rich trading grounds of the East. It is said that when the two memorials are lined up, they indicate the location of the much-feared Whittle Rock.

At Olifantsbospunt, about halfway between Cape Point and Scarborough, are the wrecks of the *Thomas T. Tucker*, which ran aground here in 1942, and the *Nolloth*, which sank in 1965 at nearby Duikerklip.

Cape Point

The southern tip of the Cape Peninsula is not, despite popular belief, the meeting place of the Indian and Atlantic oceans; this honour is reserved for Cape Agulhas, the southernmost point of Africa. Visitors will often encounter this myth, yet if ever there was a place which could be forgiven for perpetuating the myth, it is Cape Point. The natural beauty and superlative views provide one of the wonders of the peninsula, and visitors flock here – to take photographs, breathe the sea air, admire the fynbos and walk the unspoilt terrain.

Dias Beach, shielded by cliffs, may be reached only via a rugged flight of steps, but the panorama that awaits is exceptional. From Dias, the highest sea cliffs in the country tower up to the point and lighthouse. But some of the best views must surely be those from the shop and restaurant complex on the cliffs near the main parking area. From here, the views across to Muizenberg may take your breath away. The curio shop and the popular **Two Oceans Restaurant** are located here. There is also a snack bar and information desk at the lower station of the funicular railway, which ferries visitors up to the old lighthouse at the top of the point. At the top of the funicular, there is another shop, and an information centre housed in the former home of the lighthouse keeper.

The 300-metre (985 feet) cliffs fall straight down from the lookout platform above, and the view from here extends across False Bay to Danger Point, some 80 kilometres (50 miles) to the east. This is also the site of the old 2 000-candlepower lighthouse which was erected in 1861 and served for 50 years. After the Portuguese liner *Lusitania* foundered on Bellows Rock below in 1911, a second lighthouse was built further down in 1914. This new lighthouse, which was electrified in 1936, may be seen from viewpoints at the upper station.

Scarborough and Kommetjie

The sleepy seaside village of **Scarborough** is an idyllic getaway. Just beyond Scarborough is majestic **Misty Cliffs**. There are plenty of picnic areas around here, but don't miss the food at the **Camel Rock** restaurant on Main Road. The vegetarian fare and seafood are exceptional.

Between Scarborough and the Slangkoppunt lighthouse, tiny **Witsand** offers two diversions: the **crayfish factory** on Witsand Island prepares fresh seafood for export, and is open to the public by appointment; the rustic **Soetwater Recreation Camp** has no electricity, but offers facilities for overnight camping, a snack bar, caravan stands, a tidal pool and picnic spots.

Kommetjie is a little closer to what most travellers would call 'civilisation'. The little fishing village, dotted with milkwood trees, was established at the turn of the century and is a mecca for watersport enthusiasts, with surfers, waveskiers, windsurfers and fishermen flocking to the area. Like Scarborough and the rest of the southern peninsula, the natural heritage here is relatively untouched, with only a scattering of holiday homes. Apart from the magnificent

85

stretch of white sand that is Long Beach – which incorporates both Klein Slangpunt and Bokramstrand – other attractions include the Slangkop Lighthouse which dates from 1919, and the wreck of the *Kakapo*, a steamship that ran aground on its maiden voyage in 1900 when its captain made the fatal error of mistaking Chapman's Peak for Cape Point.

Imhoff's Gift, between Kommetjie/Ocean View and Noordhoek is a pleasant reminder of days gone by. Originally the property of Baron von Imhoff, Commissioner of the VOC in 1743, and who established the port at Simon's Town, the buildings have been turned into a unique community centre. There are several offbeat shops, a farmstall, tea garden and camel or horse rides for the children. The **Nature Park and Wildlife Sanctuary**, part of Hout Bay's World of Birds, houses giants of the bird world such as ostriches, emus and blue cranes. Right next door is the **Snake Park**, offering a rare close look at snakes from all over the world, in addition to spiders and a host of reptiles.

On the M65 leading from Kommetjie stands the **Masephumelele Village**. This traditional Xhosa village – the name means 'We must succeed' – is open to the public on weekends only, and both the

exhibits and the array of wares on sale are well worth a stop. See the wide range of authentic handcrafts and artworks of the Xhosa people, and enjoy the indigenous crafts by taking some home as a memento.

Silvermine Nature Reserve
The scenic route from Kommetjie and surrounds takes the traveller along Kommetjie Road towards Fish Hoek and then

Adventure Safaris & Sport Tours, tel: 438-5201
Cape Point Information Centre: tel: 780-9200.
False Bay Tourist Rendezvous: Balmoral Building, 52 Beach Rd., Muizenberg; tel: 788-6176.
Kalk Bay Harbour (harbour master): Main Rd., Kalk Bay; tel: 788-8313.
Simon's Town Publicity Association: 111 St George's St., Simon's Town; open daily 9am-4.30pm; tel: 786-2436.
Southcoast Seafaris, tel: 082 553 0185
White Shark Ecoventures, tel: 082 658 0185

PLACES OF INTEREST
Cape of Good Hope Nature Reserve: open daily 7am-6pm; entry fee; tel: 780-9100.
Cape Point Ostrich Farm: Bonne Attente Farm, Cape Point; open daily 9am-5.30pm; entry fee; tel: 780-9294.
False Bay Fire Museum: Brakloof Rd., Fish Hoek; tel: 788-1387.
Fish Hoek Valley Museum: 59 Central Circle, Fish Hoek; open Tues-Sun 9.30am-12.30pm; tel: 782-1756.
False Bay Yacht Club: King George's Way, Simon's Town; tel: 786-1703.
Het Post Huijs: Main Rd., Muizenberg; open Mon-Sat; tel: 788-7031.
Imhoff's Gift: Kommetjie Rd., Kommetjie; tel: 783-4545.
Masiphumelele Village: Main Rd., Kommetjie; open 9am-5pm Sat-Sun; tel: 387-5351.
Muizenberg Museum Complex: Main Rd., Muizenberg; tel: 788-7035.
Muizenberg Toy Museum and Collectors' Shop: 8 Beach Rd., Muizenberg, open 10am-5pm Tues-Sat, tel: 788-1569.
Natale Labia Museum: 192 Main Rd., St James; open Tues-Sun 9am-4.30pm; tel: 788-4106.
Nature Park and Wildlife Sanctuary: Ocean View Rd., Kommetjie; open daily 9am-5pm; tel: 783-2309.
Naval Dockyard (tours): West Dockyard, Simon's Town; by appointment only; tel: 787-3911.
Rhodes Cottage Museum: 246 Main Rd., Muizenberg; open Tues-Sun 10am-1pm; tel: 788-1816.
Silvermine Nature Reserve: Ou Kaapse Weg, Tokai; 8am-6pm daily; entry fee; tel: 713-0260.
Simon's Town Museum: Court Rd., Simon's Town; open Mon-Sat 9am-4pm, Sun 1pm-4pm; tel: 786-3046.
Snake Park: 783-3573
South African Naval Museum (Martello Tower): West Dockyard, Court Rd., Simon's Town; open daily 10am-4pm; tel: 787-4686.
Stempastorie Museum: 2 Church St., Simon's Town; open 9am-4.30pm Wed-Fri; tel: 786-3226.
Topstones Mineral World: Dido Valley Rd., Simon's Town; open Mon-Fri 8.30am-4.45pm, 9am-5.30pm Sat-Sun; tel: 786-2020.
Warrior Toy Museum: St George's Street, Simon's Town; open 10am-4pm; entry fee; tel: 786-1395.
Witsand Crayfish Factory: Witsand Island; tel: 783-1757.

left onto one of the most magnificent stretches of road in the Cape. Both the setting and the views along **Ou Kaapse Weg** – meaning 'Old Cape Road' – are quite extraordinary as it winds through the mountainside and into **Silvermine Nature Reserve**. The reserve covers much of what was the original silver mine initiated by Governor Simon van der Stel in 1687, when he sent prospectors on a fruitless search for the precious metal.

There are a number of points of entry from Ou Kaapse Weg into the reserve, part of which is occupied by a South African Navy base. There are braai and picnic areas, while the conservation area encompasses some of the finest expanses of fynbos vegetation and other Cape flora in the peninsula. Silvermine's wildlife includes a diversity of birds – among them the black eagle – and mammal species varying from antelopes such as grysbok and rhebok to genets, porcupines and baboons, plus an array of insects, amphibians and reptiles.

The area to the west of the Ou Kaapse Weg leads to the source of the Silvermine River – Noordhoek Peak, at about 750 metres (2 460 feet) above sea level, and the highest point in Silvermine. The panorama from here stretches along Chapman's Peak Drive to The Sentinel in Hout Bay. On the eastern side of Ou Kaapse Weg lie the mountains of Muizenberg and Kalkbaaiberg and a view which embraces False Bay, the Southern Suburbs and Constantia, Table Mountain and across the Cape Flats to the Strand. The peace that covers the land invites not only a deep admiration for its natural heritage, but also a sense of the Cape Town of old, and the experience will remain a fond memory.

OPPOSITE TOP *From the Cape Point lighthouse, visitors are afforded a spectacular view of the Cape of Good Hope.*

OPPOSITE BOTTOM *The tidal pools of Scarborough are home to large beds of the black mussels so popular on local menus.*

ABOVE *A hawker at the entrance to the Cape of Good Hope Nature Reserve displays a contemporary angle on traditional wire craft.*

Constantia &
The Southern Suburbs

Day Six

CONSTANTIA & THE SOUTHERN SUBURBS

Rhodes Memorial · Rosebank · Rondebosch · Newlands · Claremont · Wynberg · Constantia
Groot Constantia · Constantia Nek · Rondevlei Nature Reserve

The Southern Suburbs lie in the shadow of the mountain ranges which form the spine of the peninsula. Situated in what is known as the Green Belt – the average rainfall at the foot of the mountains tends to be higher than in the rest of the Cape – the lush suburbs provide not only a peek at Capetonians at home, but also a revealing look into the history of the city itself, particularly during the days of English and Dutch occupation. As a result, this string of residential areas reflects a broad and eclectic combination of influences, mixing magnificent Cape Dutch architecture with the Georgian and Victorian styles brought from England.

Access routes to the suburbs at the foot of Table Mountain are plentiful and varied. From the city, take either Eastern Boulevard or De Waal Drive – the latter changes its name regularly along the route, but follow the signs for the Southern Suburbs. As its name implies, Main Road is an important (if sometimes crowded and slow) route, which snakes through most of the Southern Suburbs. From the False Bay area, take the Blue Route (the M3 highway).

On his death in 1906, Cecil John Rhodes, premier of the Cape Colony, left the Rhodes Estate on the eastern slopes of Table Mountain to the nation. The land originally extended to the site of today's Groote Schuur Hospital, and includes such famed landmarks as Mostert's Mill, Rhodes Memorial and the Groote Schuur manor house.

The Slopes of Table Mountain

Travelling from the city to the suburbs on De Waal Drive past Devil's Peak, an expanse of open land stretches up the slopes. This is a closed nature reserve, and on sunny days small herds of grazing mountain zebra and wildebeest dot the landscape, unperturbed by the city traffic on the highway below.

Perhaps the most famous structure on this portion of the mountain is the grand monument built in commemoration of Cecil John Rhodes. Rhodes was only 18 when he and his brother staked their first claims on the diamond fields of Kimberley, but by the time he died he had created the world's most successful mining house, amassed an immense fortune,

---

PREVIOUS PAGES *The rural solitude of Buitenverwachting makes it the ideal setting for one of the Cape's most respected restaurants.*

INSET *Many of the famed old homesteads of Constantia are dated by the distinctive gables of the manor houses.*

ABOVE *The verandah-enclosed shrine of Sayed Mahmud is situated on the summit of Constantia's tranquil Islam Hill.*

OPPOSITE *Shrouded in lush greenery, 200-year-old Klein Constantia is one of the peninsula's premier wine estates.*

and even given his name to a country (Rhodesia, now Zimbabwe), acquiring along the way a reputation as a ruthless businessman, imperialist and politician.

The temple-like **Rhodes Memorial** was executed by Sir Herbert Baker in grand neo-Classical style, and was constructed in 1912 from Table Mountain granite. The centrepiece of the upper, colonnaded section is J.W. Swan's bust of Rhodes, inscribed with the words penned by Rudyard Kipling in honour of the statesman. At the foot of the monument's stone steps, which are guarded by eight massive bronze lions, stands an impressive equestrian statue, titled 'Physical Energy', and sculpted by G.F. Watts. The view from the steps is quite breathtaking, taking in the city and immediate suburbs below, the Cape Flats, Tygerberg Hills and the distant Hottentots-Holland Mountains.

Tucked away behind the memorial and surrounded by the mountain's unique flora, stands a charming old stone cottage which serves as a restaurant and tearoom. The tiny lodge is particularly popular for afternoon tea and as a venue for intimate receptions. Just a little further up the slopes of the mountain, a small Prayer Garden is open to the public.

Below Rhodes Memorial, visitors will notice the characteristic sails of a traditional Dutch windmill at the turn-off from Rhodes Drive into Woolsack Drive, which leads down the hill into the suburb of Rosebank. This is **Mostert's Mill**, a rare example of an authentic Dutch windmill. The mill was built in 1796 by Wouter Mostert, one of the small number of free burghers who were permitted by Commander Jan van Riebeeck to establish farms beyond the immediate confines of the settlement on Table Bay. The mill was later purchased by the Van Reenen family of the farm Welgelegen. With financial aid from the Netherlands, the structure was painstakingly restored in 1936 and today Mostert's Mill is open to the public.

Observatory to Rosebank

The **South African Astronomical Observatory**, located off Observatory Road, has given its name to the bohemian suburb of Observatory. Built in 1820, the facility hosts plenty of activities related to the observation of the skies, and offers guided tours of the observatory itself. At eight o'clock every second Saturday, the observatory invites visitors to watch the stars over the city through its telescope.

The **Irma Stern Museum** on Cecil Road in Rosebank is a satellite of the University of Cape Town's fine art department, and provides considerable insight into the work and life of one of South Africa's most gifted painters. More than 200 of her paintings are exhibited in the house, which was her home for nearly 40 years. Born in Germany, Irma Stern was at times a controversial figure, but her passionate brushstrokes and exciting use of colour have ensured that her work remains highly regarded and much sought after. The museum also houses her collections of African, European and Eastern art and furniture, which she accumulated during her extensive travels. Her studio – which has been left undisturbed since her death in 1966 – is also the venue for temporary exhibitions of contemporary art.

OPPOSITE *The columned grandeur of Rhodes Memorial is an impressive reminder of one of the country's key historical figures.*

ABOVE *The view over Cape Town and its suburbs from Rhodes Memorial is undeniably inspiring.*

RIGHT *Sculpted by G.F. Watts, the statue of 'Physical Energy' stands boldly in the centre of the memorial to Rhodes.*

Rondebosch

Almost around the corner from the Irma Stern Museum, off Woolsack Drive on the Main Road, stands the University of Cape Town's **Baxter Theatre Complex**. Built nearly 20 years ago, the Baxter's theatres are the venue for the most prominent local stage productions. The main theatre concentrates on the more lavish and spectacular shows and musicals; performances in the concert hall vary from dramatic productions to popular and classical music recitals, while the Studio hosts experimental drama and cabarets. The foyer often exhibits local art, and there is both a restaurant and bar catering largely for the after-theatre crowd. Unfortunately, the Baxter's two cinemas – which often screened art films rarely seen by the South African public – have now closed.

The most prominent landmark in the Rondebosch/Rosebank area – and, indeed, in the whole of the Southern Suburbs – is the **University of Cape Town**, the academic home of some 15 000 students. This array of sandstone buildings stands on the slopes of Devil's Peak, and houses the upper campus of South Africa's oldest university.

The other great landmark in Rondebosch is, of course, **Groote Schuur**. Meaning 'great barn', the Cape Dutch manor house was originally built by Jan van Riebeeck in which to store the colony's all-important grain supply. When Cecil John Rhodes bought the granary, he had Sir Herbert Baker execute the renovations which we see today. The mansion – which is not open to the public – still houses the artworks and texts left behind by Rhodes for the nation.

As you travel further south, Main Road seems to split, creating a small 'island' in the middle of the road. On the left is the Riverside shopping centre and the old Rondebosch Fountain, a charming reminder of the ornate Victorian era. On the right, in the centre of the island, stands the stone chapel of **St Paul's Anglican Church**.

Newlands

Home to the country's most famous playing fields, the green suburb of Newlands, like much of the Southern Suburbs, is lined with avenues of oaks and is sheltered by the great bulk of the mountain. Through the tranquil suburb winds the Liesbeek River, along the banks of which stands the **Josephine Mill** on Boundary Road. Built in 1840, The mill is Cape Town's only surviving operational water mill; the cast-iron wheel was built by Jacob Letterstedt in the same year the mill started operation. Today, the Josephine Mill is the headquarters of the Cape Town Historical Society, but continues to produce the flour for which

it was originally built. Visitors can purchase flour ground on the premises and, of course, baked goods. Open to the public throughout the year, the Josephine Mill and its tea garden are popular venues for summertime concerts. Because of its lush and serene setting, it is also a much-favoured venue for intimate wedding receptions.

Boundary Road is also home to the **Rugby Museum** – one of the oldest of its kind in the world – which houses a valuable collection of rugby souvenirs and collectibles dating as far back as 1891. A more contemporary sporting shrine is nearby **Norwich Park** – formerly known as the Newlands cricket and rugby grounds. As the headquarters of the Western Province Rugby Union and the Western Province Cricket Union, Norwich Park is the setting for exciting international rugby and cricket test matches. In recent years Norwich Park has also been the venue for major pop concerts – Tina Turner and Cliff Richard have numbered among the performers – and other important public events.

ABOVE *Sprawled across the slopes of the mountain lie the ivy-bedecked landmark buildings of the University of Cape Town.*

OPPOSITE *Approximately 15 000 students have chosen the esteemed University of Cape Town as their seat of learning.*

Along Main Road towards Claremont and beyond, visitors will see – and likely smell the fermenting hops – the premises of **South African Breweries**, one of the country's largest and most successful business enterprises. Just a little further, in Colinton Road (off Main Road) is the majestic **Vineyard Hotel**. Built in the last year of the eighteenth century and imbued with all the elegance of the period, this gracious structure was christened 'Paradise' by its initial owners, Lord Andrew Barnard and his wife Lady Anne – who acted as the official hostess at the Cape during the absence of the wife of the governor, Earl Macartney.

Claremont

Covering what was once the Weltevreden Estate, the suburb of **Claremont** is a place of contrasts. The leafy streets are clearly the domain of the wealthy, yet along Main Road the pavements teem with informal street vendors, and impromptu stalls sprawl across the pavements. But the suburb is also home to **Cavendish Square**, one of the country's finest and most exclusive shopping complexes. Recently renovated, the plush interior of Cavendish Square comprises upmarket boutiques, restaurants (including a

McDonald's outlet) and cinemas. Adjacent to the complex are equally sophisticated stores in **Cavendish Close** and **The Link**.

For a pleasant break from shopping, take a stroll through Claremont's **Arderne Gardens**, the Victorian park laid out by Ralph Henry Arderne in 1845, situated on Main Road. The green oasis along the main artery of the suburbs offers a chance to rest and relax. Arderne Gardens boasts not only a variety of indigenous and exotic flora, but also a tranquil formal garden laid out in Japanese style. These gardens are particularly popular with wedding parties, who gather for photographs in the shade of the cypress, cedar, and pine trees.

Wynberg

To the south of Claremont is **Kenilworth**, home to the Kenilworth Racecourse and venue for the J&B Metropolitan Handicap, one of the most prestigious horse races on the sport and social calendar. Beyond Kenilworth, though, is **Wynberg**, located on a hill that was once part of Van Riebeeck's original farm Bosch Heuwel. Because it was planted with vines to serve as the governor's personal vineyard, it became known as Wynberg, or 'wine mountain'. Once a

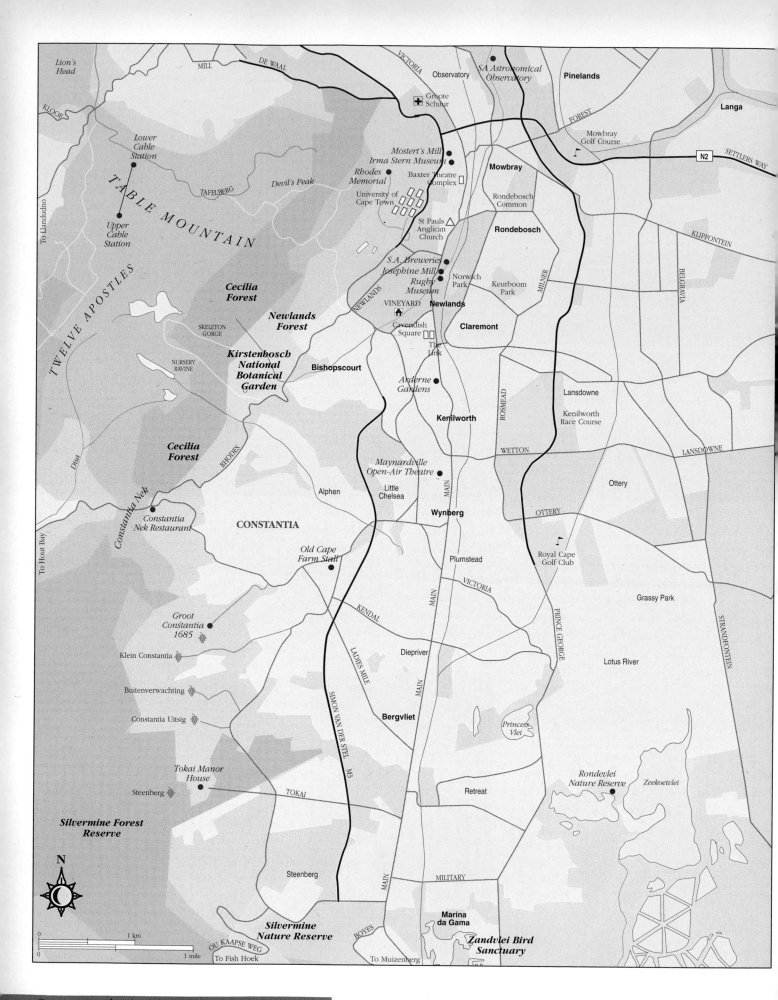

Lion's Head

KLOOF

MILL

DE WAAL

VICTORIA

Observatory

S.A. Astronomical Observatory

Pinelands

Langa

Groote Schuur

TAFELBERG

Devil's Peak

Lower Cable Station

Mostert's Mill
Irma Stern Museum

Baxter Theatre Complex

Mowbray

FOREST

Mowbray Golf Course

N2

SETTLERS WAY

To Llandudno

T A B L E   M O U N T A I N

Upper Cable Station

Rhodes Memorial

University of Cape Town

Rondebosch Common

St Pauls Anglican Church

Rondebosch

KLIPFONTEIN

BELGRAVIA

T W E L V E   A P O S T L E S

Cecilia Forest

SKELETON GORGE

Newlands Forest

NURSERY RAVINE

S.A. Breweries
Josephine Mill
Rugby Museum

Norwich Park

Keurboom Park

MILNER

NEWLANDS

VINEYARD

Newlands

Claremont

Kirstenbosch National Botanical Garden

Cavendish Square

The Link

Bishopscourt

Arderne Gardens

ROSMEAD

Lansdowne

Kenilworth Race Course

Cecilia Forest

RHODES

DISA

Maynardville Open-Air Theatre

Kenilworth

WETTON

LANSDOWNE

Ottery

Constantia Nek

Constantia Nek Restaurant

Alphen

Little Chelsea

MAIN

Wynberg

OTTERY

Old Cape Farm Stall

CONSTANTIA

Plumstead

Royal Cape Golf Club

PRINCE GEORGE

VICTORIA

Grassy Park

STRANDFONTEIN

Groot Constantia 1685

KENDAL

MAIN

Dieprivier

Lotus River

Klein Constantia

LADIES MILE

Buitenverwachting

Constantia Uitsig

SIMON VAN DER STEL

M3

Bergvliet

Princess Vlei

Tokai Manor House

Steenberg

Rondevlei Nature Reserve

Zeekoeivlei

Silvermine Forest Reserve

TOKAI

Retreat

N

Steenberg

MAIN

MILITARY

Silvermine Nature Reserve

BOYES

Marina da Gama

OU KAAPSE WEG
To Fish Hoek

Zandvlei Bird Sanctuary

To Muizenberg

0 — 1 km
0 — 1 mile

To Hout Bay

tranquil village, Wynberg is now a bustling modern suburb and its principal thoroughfare is lined with shops and large department stores. Wynberg is noted for its old cottages – particularly in the neighbourhood known as **Little Chelsea**. Although some cottages have been restored as business premises, others have now become sought-after real estate.

Wynberg's greatest treasure must surely be the **Maynardville Open-Air Theatre**, which presents Shakespearean productions during the balmy summer months. Theatregoers may enjoy the works of the Bard under the still night sky, and picnic on the lawns beside the small lake before the performance. Reservations may be made through Computicket. Alongside the theatre, on an expanse of ground known simply as Maynardville, the representatives of charity organisations gather annually in February to host the **Community Chest Carnival**. The proceeds of the three-day event are awarded to deserving charities, and thousands of Capetonians flock to the grounds to wander amid the stalls representing the nations of the world.

Winelands of the Peninsula

South Africa is known the world over for its fine wines, but most of the Cape's wineries lie some distance inland of Cape Town. The exception is, of course, the vineyards across the hills and vales of **Constantia** – where the country's very first vines were planted. The valleys of this prestigious residential area are lush with woods and parklands. The hills and forest glades abound with flora, making Constantia popular among hikers and horse riders. Access to the Constantia winelands is via either Constantia Road from Wynberg or Rhodes Drive from Kirstenbosch Botanic Gardens. The latter road is also a favourite for those who wish to take in the lavish exteriors of the homes of the rich and famous.

Constantia's Wine Estates

Travelling from Wynberg on Constantia Road, visitors first encounter the **Alphen Estate**, which dates back to 1714. Unfortunately, wine is no longer produced here, although it is distributed under the Alphen label. The first owner, Willem Adriaan van der Stel, did not incorporate the Alphen lands into

ABOVE *The rural tranquillity of the Constantia Valley belies its proximity to the city centre.*

his personal estate, and so the vineyards were granted to Theunis van Schalkwyk. Nearly 35 years later, in 1748, Abraham Lever erected the Georgian manor house which is today the Alphen Hotel. The hotel is now the property of Peter Bairnsfather Cloete, a descendant of Hendrick Cloete, the first owner of the Groot Constantia estate.

Steenberg, the oldest farm in the area, lies on the mountain slopes at the southern end of the valley. Located on the corner of Steenberg and Tokai roads, the farm was granted by Simon van der Stel to Catharina Ras in 1688. The homestead was erected by Frederick Rossouw in 1695. In 1990, the land was purchased by a mining company, Johannesburg Consolidated Investments. An exclusive golf club and housing complex has been laid out and investors are intent on recreating the once prominent wine estate. Fine wines continue to be made here, although sales are by appointment only. Although the recently opened Steenberg restaurant is not quite in the same league as other famed eateries in the area – such as Buitenverwachting and Uitsig – its unusual combination of Cape Dutch architecture, high-tech European interior styling and Thai cuisine offers an intriguing and thoroughly contemporary dining experience.

Although not devoted to wine-making, the **Tokai Manor House** on Tokai Road is worth a visit, if only to see a superb example of period architecture. The mansion, with its Thibault-designed facade and traditional *stoep*, or verandah, was built by Andries Teubes in 1795. Because it is a private home, Tokai Manor House is not open to visitors.

Situated some distance north, on the slopes of the Constantiaberg, is **Buitenverwachting** ('beyond expectations'). The name is fitting, for the estate is home to one of the very best of the city's top restaurants, and boasts an outstanding menu of Cape cuisine. The gabled home, along with its cellars and original slave quarters and stables, have all been faithfully restored, and the estate today produces an excellent selection of wines. Although tours of the prized cellars are exclusively by

appointment, the nominal fee charged on entry includes a taste of the estate's wine. Buitenverwachting also hosts summer concerts, and is particularly known for its popular jazz recitals. Picnickers are advised to take their own buffet, as the restaurant does not offer this service.

Located on the Spaanschemat River Road, and adjacent to Buitenverwachting, is the **Constantia Uitsig** farm, also noted for fine dining. Set among the vineyards of the horsey set, the Uitsig manor was originally the accommodation for the estate's horses, but today the stables have been converted into a graceful hotel, with both a cricket pavilion and a superb restaurant.

Tours of the 200-year-old **Klein Constantia** estate nearby are by appointment only, but for visitors keen to sample some of the best of the Cape wines, it is certainly worth the effort. The homestead remains faithful to its historic past, and there are a number of interesting diversions. Within the grounds of Klein Constantia stands a *kramat*, or Muslim shrine, dedicated to one of the last sultans banished to the colony from Malacca by the Dutch in the late 1660s.

Constantia

In Constantia proper, the famed **Old Cape Farmstall** is within walking distance of the Groot Constantia estate. Much more than just a roadside fruit and vegetable market, the farmstall is a local institution. Set amid towering oak trees, it also boasts a good restaurant and other shops. The fare includes an array of home-baked and prepared goodies – ideal for stocking up the picnic basket. Here, too, are the offices of the High Constantia Touring Company, which takes visitors through the Groot Constantia winelands in a horse-drawn coach. Naturally, the half-hour or hour experience does not come cheaply, but it may be worth the extra few rands to see the vineyards from a carriage.

Just behind the Old Cape Farmstall, on the Groot Constantia Road to the left, is the wine estate originally owned by Governor Simon van der Stel. After his death in 1712, the land was subdivided into Groot Constantia, Bergvliet and Klein Constantia. Groot Constantia was later divided yet again and a portion was renamed Klein Constantia. Because of the inevitable confusion, the small estate became known as Hoop op Constantia, and it is still known as such today. The original

OPPOSITE TOP *Charming Constantia Uitsig is the home of a renowned restaurant.*

OPPOSITE BOTTOM *The vineyards of Groot Constantia are among the few within the peninsula that continue to produce wine.*

ABOVE *Faithful to its historic past, the grand old Groot Constantia manor house symbolizes Constantia's wine-making heritage.*

99

Bergvliet farm was also subdivided and the wine-producing land was renamed Buitenverwachting. Together with Groot Constantia and Klein Constantia, the privately owned Buitenverwachting forms part of Cape Town's only wine route.

Groot Constantia

The ground on which the suburb of Constantia now stands was presented to Governor Simon van der Stel by Commissioner van Rhede in 1685. Magnificent **Groot Constantia** boasts the country's oldest manor house, with a vineyard that was planted by Van der Stel in 1685 – the same year the mansion was erected. In 1778, the gabled and thatched mansion passed into the hands of the Cloete family, the country's most prominent vintners. Patriarch Hendrick Cloete commissioned architect Louis Thibault and master sculptor Anton Anreith to conduct renovations, among them the addition of a two-storey cellar and a pediment sculpted with Greek gods and cherubs. Thibault's cellar today serves as a wine museum, while the traditional high-ceilinged rooms of the manor house itself – restored after it was destroyed by fire in 1925 – houses a choice collection of period furniture and objets d'art. The nearby Jonkershuis, traditional home of the family's eldest son destined to inherit the estate, served until recently as a restaurant offering typical Cape dishes. Today, however, it is

USEFUL INFORMATION

Alphen Hotel: Alphen Drive, Constantia; tel: 794-5011.

Baxter Theatre Complex: Main Road, Rosebank; tel: 685-7880.

Buitenverwachting: Spaanschemat River Road, Constantia; open 9am-5pm; tel: 794-5190.

Constantia Uitsig: Spaanschemat River Rd, Constantia; tel: 794-4480.

Groot Constantia: Groot Constantia Road, Constantia; open daily 10am-5pm; tel: 794-1144.

Irma Stern Museum: Cecil Road, Rosebank; open Tues-Sat 10am-5pm; tel: 685-5686.

Josephine Mill: Boundary Road, Newlands; open 9am-4pm; tel: 686-4939.

Klein Constantia: Spaanschemat River Road, Constantia; open 10am-5pm; tel: 794-5188.

Maynardville Open-Air Theatre: cnr Church/Wolfe streets, Wynberg.

Mostert's Mill: Rhodes Drive, Rondebosch; open daily 9am-3pm.

Old Cape Farmstall: Main Road, Constantia; open daily 8.30am-7pm; tel: 794-7062/3.

Rhodes Memorial: Rhodes Drive, Rondebosch; tel: 689-9151.

Rondevlei Bird Sanctuary: Perth Road, Grassy Park; open daily 8am-5pm; tel: 706-2404.

Rugby Museum: Boundary Road, Newlands; open daily 9am-3pm; entry fee; tel: 685-3038.

South African Astronomical Observatory: Liesbeek Parkway, Observatory; tel: 447-0025.

South African Breweries (Ohlsson's Cape Breweries): Boundary Road, Newlands: open Mon-Thurs 9.15am-4.45pm; tel: 658-7255/7511.

Steenberg Estate: cnr Steenberg/Tokai roads, Tokai; tel: 713-2222 (Country Hotel & Restaurant); tel: 713-2233 (Golf Estate).

Vineyard Hotel: Colinton Road, Newlands; tel: 683-3044.

used as the cellar of the modern wine-making operation, which offers both tours and tastings. There is also an intimate gallery of contemporary art and a busy souvenir shop.

The estate's Tavern is an informal eatery serving light meals and pub lunches either under the timber beams of the barn-like interior or under the sunny Cape skies. The surrounding grounds offer splendid views of the wineland, and are ideal for relaxing picnic lunches – and a bottle of the estate wine.

Constantia Nek

At the summit of Constantia Nek – the pass that links Constantia with Hout Bay – stands the 70-year-old **Constantia Nek Restaurant**, one of Cape Town's oldest and most highly regarded eateries. With its gabled exterior and panelled interior, the Constantia Nek Restaurant remains a favourite spot for diners – the huge hearth is particularly cosy on winter evenings. On the verge outside, you may want to purchase an original watercolour depicting scenes of the peninsula.

Rondevlei Nature Reserve

Although not officially part of the Southern Suburbs, the **Rondevlei Nature Reserve** is nevertheless one of the city's most fascinating wild areas. The reserve is located on Perth Road in Grassy Park, and boasts an enormous variety of Cape fauna, as well as lookout points, hides and viewing towers equipped with telescopes. There is even a walkway edging the waters of the lagoon. Rondevlei is home to about 225 species of birds, including many water birds, but is perhaps equally well known for its resident pygmy hippos. There is also a small museum that details the history of the reserve.

OPPOSITE TOP Famed not only for its fine wines, Groot Constantia's restaurant serves up an interesting and varied menu.

OPPOSITE BOTTOM The cool, high-ceilinged interior of the Groot Constantia manor house is furnished with old Cape pieces.

TOP The charming Constantia Nek Restaurant has become a fixture in the hearts of Capetonians.

ABOVE Pelicans take off from the tranquil waters of Rondevlei Nature Reserve.

Constantia & The Southern Suburbs

Stellenbosch

Day Seven

$\mathcal{S}$TELLENBOSCH

The Early Days • University Town • Dorp Street • Monuments and Museums • Village Museum
Arts and Entertainment • Visitors' Stellenbosch • Flora and Fauna • The Wine Industry

Although not strictly within the confines of the city of Cape Town, a visit to the Fairest Cape is incomplete without an excursion to some of the surrounding communities and wine estates. Of the three wine 'routes', or districts, located in the vicinity of Cape Town, the best known of these centres on the university town of Stellenbosch (the other wine routes being Paarl and Franschhoek). Located 48 kilometres (30 miles) east of Cape Town, South Africa's second oldest town is steeped in history and a proud contributor to the country's renowned wine industry.

The Early Days

The 300-year-old town at the foot of Papegaaiberg (Parrot Mountain) started out as a farming community – originally intended by the Dutch East India Company (VOC) to supply fresh fruit and vegetables for company ships on their way to and from the East – and was the first settlement to be established beyond the immediate boundaries of the Cape colony. Named after Governor Simon van der Stel, who initiated the planting

of the many oaks which line the old streets – hence the nickname Eikestad, meaning 'oak town' – Stellenbosch has played an important role in the history of the country and is home to many museums and national monuments which explore this heritage.

One of the town's most prominent buildings is the gabled **Moederkerk** (Mother Church) on Drostdy Street. Its predecessor, consecrated in 1687, originally stood in Church Street where D'Ouwe Werf stands today. The church was central to the community, and also served as the principal place of worship for the Huguenots, French Protestant refugees who settled in the district after fleeing religious persecution in their home country. The first church was destroyed by fire in 1710, and its cross-shaped replacement was finally reconsecrated on the new site in 1723. The original Baroque gable and thatched roof was replaced in 1806 with neo-Classical innovations when the new church was renovated and enlarged to accommodate the growing congregation. Today the church is a reminder of the past, and a modern place of worship.

PREVIOUS PAGES *Victorian cottages along oak-lined Dorp Street evoke Stellenbosch's rich architectural heritage.*

INSET *In a district blessed with rich soils and bountiful harvests, strawberry picking is a favourite holiday pastime.*

ABOVE *Stellenbosch's unique Toy and Miniature Museum is housed in a handsome Cape Dutch structure.*

OPPOSITE *Above the placid waters of Jonkershoek rises a spectacular backdrop of mountain and forest.*

University Town

Although considered the centre of the wine industry, Stellenbosch is also renowned for its academic institutions. The first seminary opened its doors in 1859, and the University of Stellenbosch was established in 1918. These were later followed by the founding of a number of schools and colleges.

ABOVE *Spilling out onto the filigreed verandah of Oom Samie se Winkel is just a fraction of the treasures which lie inside.*

LEFT *Delightful Oom Samie se Winkel is filled to the eaves with archaic implements, farm goods and handmade crafts.*

OPPOSITE *Sunlight filters into the cool interior of the NG Moederkerk through its stained-glass windows.*

Dorp Street

The heart of old Stellenbosch is **Dorp Street**, the monument-lined thoroughfare punctuated by venerable oak trees and ornate Victorian townhouses. The former wagon road remains true to its origins and is unblemished by the trappings of a modern city: even the narrow canals which supplied water to the early homes remain intact.

Among the best-preserved structures on the street are: **Bakker House**, home of sailor and missionary Jans Bakker, who taught slaves here; the gabled home at 149 Dorp Street – the date on the gable misleadingly refers only to the year the gable was added; and other typical town homes, such as those found at numbers 151, 155, and 159 Dorp Street.

Undoubtedly the most famous of all Dorps Street's quaint buildings is **Oom Samie se Winkel**, the local general dealer, which dates back to 1904. The old Victorian-style shop stocks an enormous variety of goods, ranging from lacework and dried fish to second-hand ornaments and household implements, but the proprietors are also wine merchants and exporters who will arrange to have visitors' purchases sent abroad if required.

Also on Dorp Street is the Gothic-style **Old Lutheran Church**, also designed by Carl Otto Hager – who lived at De Eiken on Market Street – and dating from 1851. Today the church accommodates the University of Stellenbosch's art

One of the most significant of these seats of education was the **Ou Hoofgebou** on Ryneveld Street. Designed in Classical style by Carl Hager – the German artist who oversaw the renovations of the Moederkerk – construction of the college began in 1879 to commemorate the town's bicentenary. It finally opened its doors in 1886 as Victoria College. The fine facade includes a pediment depicting the institution's coat of arms supported by lions, a colonnaded verandah, an ornamental balcony and impressive fanlights over the upper windows.

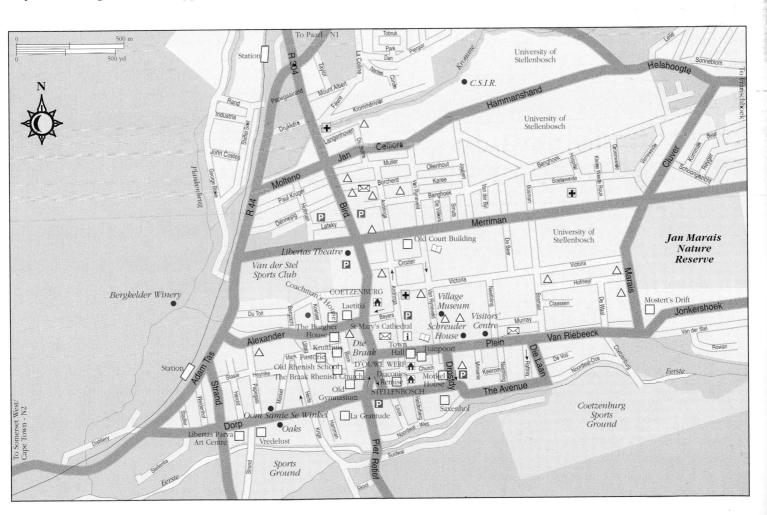

gallery and is open from Monday to Saturday. Visitors should note that, like the art gallery, few shops and public buildings in towns like Stellenbosch are open on Sundays, and liquor may still not be sold on these days.

The graceful building of **Libertas Parva** was the home of the wife of statesman, naturalist and soldier Jan Christiaan Smuts. Today it houses the **Rembrandt van Rijn Art Museum**, one of the country's finest private art collections, which includes works by sculptor Anton van Wouw and painter Irma Stern.

Alongside Libertas Parva stands the **Stellenryck Wine Museum**, a gabled Cape Dutch manor house dedicated to the district's wine-making tradition. From the old wine press outside to the fascinating collection of wine implements and paraphernalia such as old vats, glass bottles, corking equipment inside, the entire history of Cape wines is displayed here. Also exhibited are artefacts from Biblical times and drinking accoutrements from ancient Britain, Europe and the East.

Monuments and Museums

True to its heritage, Stellenbosch boasts an unsurpassed conglomeration of national monuments and museums dedicated to the town and the country's past. Overlooking the green expanse of **Die Braack** is the country's most fascinating – and one of the most authentic – restoration developments, known as the **Rhenish Complex**, which boasts a fine accumulation of period furniture dating back to the early days of the Cape. This complex of Cape Dutch and English-style

buildings on Bloem Street is the home of the **Tourist and Information Centre**, and includes within its precincts the Kruithuis, the Rhenish Institute and Church, the Burgerhuis and, beyond Bloem Street, Leipoldt House and the slave houses in Market Street.

The **Rhenish Church** was built in 1832 by the local missionary society as a school for the community's slaves and was opened by the governor of the Cape, Lord Charles Somerset. Lundt's ornately carved pulpit which may be seen inside, was transferred from the Moederkerk on Drostdy Street.

The whitewashed stone of the **VOC Kruithuis** – or 'powder house' – was erected in 1777 as the company's arsenal and gunpowder store. The walls are two feet thick and the roof is vaulted for added protection. The building, which features a neo-Classical bell-tower, is no longer used as a powder magazine, but its military origins are still reflected in the

ABOVE *The campus of Stellenbosch University nestles in the heart of the old town.*

OPPOSITE TOP *The Oude Libertas Amphitheatre is a relaxed venue for summertime concerts.*

OPPOSITE BOTTOM *Cannon of yesteryear and other weapons are displayed in the Kruithuis, the town's former arsenal.*

intriguing display of weaponry, arms and VOC equipment of the Dutch period and beyond.

Die Burgerhuis was built by Antonie Fick in the year 1797 and purchased by Rhenish missionary Paul Lückhoff as a parsonage in 1839. The derelict home passed into the hands of the municipality in 1952, and was restored to its original appearance. Today it houses the offices of Historical Homes of South Africa, under whose auspices the renovation of the historic Rhenish Complex were carefully undertaken.

The small houses along **Herte Street** have undergone extensive alterations since they were erected in 1834 for freed slaves and their families. Despite the passage of the years, these homes give some idea of what the streets of Stellenbosch looked like during the 1800s.

The Village Museum

Centred around Ryneveld Street, an accumulation of historic structures covers nearly five square kilometres (two square miles) of historic Stellenbosch and makes up the acclaimed **Village Museum**. Several of the town's old homesteads, ranging in style from Cape Dutch and Victorian to Regency and Georgian and which now form part of the extensive complex, have been carefully restored and refurbished according to the period. Together with their period garden landscapes, these houses are open to the public.

The 1709 **Schreuderhuis** is the oldest private home in Stellenbosch and – together with Morkel House – is the only existing building to appear on the original 1710 town blueprints. Although rather sparsely furnished, with rugged timber beams and floors of dried cattle dung, this significant period home – which survived a devastating fire in 1710 and many subsequent alterations – was painstakingly restored after remnants of the original frame were rediscovered during the process of its reconstruction.

Equally historic is **Blettermanhuis** which, with De Witt House, is the only historically important house still standing in Plein Street. The impressive H-plan house, with its six gables, was built in 1789 by Hendrik Bletterman, the last VOC-appointed *landdrost* (magistrate) to serve the town of Stellenbosch. Following his death in 1824, it became the town's police station but, in the mid-1980s, the house was converted into a museum depicting the home and lifestyle of a well-to-do Dutch family of the late 1700s.

Another home which offers some insight into the day-to-day lives of early South Africans is **Grosvenor House**. Although the current building dates back to the early 1800s, the original home was built in 1792 by Christian Neethling and then purchased seven years later by Willem Herold, who converted it to serve as his town home, adding the traditional sash windows and Classical facade and pillars. In 1876, the home became known as Grosvenor House and served as a boarding house until 1941, when it was bought by the Dutch Reformed Church. Today it exemplifies the decor and ambience of a patrician Cape family home of the early 19th century, and houses an exhibition devoted to the 'Toys of Yesteryear'.

The thatched **Ryneveld Street home** of explorer Oloff Bergh, and then of John Murray and his family, has also seen some extensions over the years. These have included the addition of a second storey, a triangular gable, the existing stone adornments on the facade and the Georgian-style sash windows – all carried out largely by the Berghs. After the much-changed house passed to Murray, however, it was transformed into a typical Victorian home, with heavy furniture, luxurious woodwork and daintily patterned wall coverings.

The offices, shop and restaurant of the Village Museum itself are situated in the Van der Bijl family home at number 37 Market Street, a beautiful old Georgian home erected after the 1803 fire. The **Van der Bijl-Huis** still retains much of its original character and houses many of the personal effects, artwork

and furnishings of the family. In the future, the Village Museum plans to add an Edwardian home and a typical 1920s-style residence, peopled by characters in authentic period costume, to the present complex.

Arts and Entertainment

The Dutch neo-Renaissance building of the **Sasol Art Museum** on Ryneveld Street was once a seat of learning, erected in 1907 as the Bloemhof School for Girls. Today, however, the red-brick building is the permanent home of the University of Stellenbosch's extensive art collection.

But there is much more to Stellenbosch than fine arts and national monuments. Just a few minutes from the town centre is the **Oude Libertas Centre** on Libertas Farm – named for the release of its original owner, Adam Tas, from a year-long prison sentence for exposing the corruption of Governor Willem Adriaan van der Stel and other company officials. Today the centre, with its underground cellar and respected restaurant, is the home of Stellenbosch Farmers' Winery (SFW), one of the

biggest wine-making conglomerates in the world. The centre's **Vinothèque** offers tours, wine sales and tastings of the award-winning wines. Guided tours tell the story of wine from the grape to the bottle and the visit includes a look at the carved oak vats in the maturation cellars, as well as demonstrations of cooperage and other crafts at the offices of SFW across the road.

Oude Libertas Centre also boasts impressive conference facilities, with audio-visual equipment, a training room, and a 100-seat theatre for presentations, while meals for the delegates are served at the Oude Libertas Restaurant. The Cape Wine Academy is also situated here, and offers courses on wine appreciation and understanding the terminology and production process.

The **Oude Libertas Amphitheatre**, built on the slope of a hill and girded by pine trees, is an intimate auditorium seating about 400 people, and the principal entertainment venue in Stellenbosch. The small amphitheatre hosts a variety of musical and dramatic productions in the open air, and Sunday evening concerts are particularly popular, especially in the balmy

the venerable **D'Ouwe Werf**. The latter, first used as an inn in 1802, is said to be the oldest established tavern in the country, and the remains of the original foundation may be viewed in the cellars below.

Apart from the historic centre of Dorp Street and its immediate surrounds, Stellenbosch offers much more. One of the best ways to see the town and its attractions is by foot. Inquire at the **Tourist and Information Centre** or the **Stellenbosch Tourist Bureau** for up-to-date information.

The village green – known as Die Braack – once served as a military parade ground, and is still a gathering place. September sees the **Stellenbosch Festival**, a feast of arts and music in celebration of the town's founding, and also the **Simon van der Stel Festival**, a pageant in which the townsfolk, students and visitors participate with gusto, while the **Stellenbosch Food and Wine Festival** is held during the last week of October.

For the dedicated shopper, there are plenty of opportunities in Stellenbosch. In some cases, prices may be higher than what you would expect to pay at home – especially during the peak tourist season – but the variety and novelty value of the purchase may be worth the few extra rands. Home and cottage industries abound, especially on the outer limits of the town. Buyers may expect to find expert knitters and weavers, spinners and potters. The best of the latter may be found at **Jean Craig Pottery** on Devon Valley Road, where potters may be seen working at their wheels. **Dombeya Farm** specialises in crafts such as handspinning and knitting. The farm occupies a scenic hillside setting a short distance from the junction of Annandale and Strand roads. Dombeya also has a pleasant tea garden – a welcome respite from the often searing summer heat. Stellenbosch also hosts a **Winelands Craft Market**, held on Sundays during the summer months.

One of the favourite excursions in the Stellenbosch area is the strawberry picking which takes place in the spring. Head for the strawberry fields adjacent to the **Mooiberge Strawberry Farmstall** – look out for the enthusiastic pickers amid the colourful scarecrows just off the road – and the strawberry patches at the **Polkadraai Farm Stall**.

Flora and Fauna

The area around Stellenbosch is blessed with a rich and varied natural heritage. Hikers will certainly want to explore the **Vineyard Hiking Trail**, which starts from the Oude Libertas Amphitheatre. From Somerset West, the **Helderberg Farm Hiking Trail** also offers a fine hiking experience. Both wind through the **Jonkershoek State Forest**. The valley of the same name, which lies sandwiched between the Jonkershoek Mountain and

evenings from December to March. Concert guests may sit in the amphitheatre or picnic on the surrounding lawns, listening to indigenous South African music, the classics – world-renowned tenor Luciano Pavarotti has performed here – or jazz. Reservations may be made through Computicket.

Visitors' Stellenbosch

Nestled among Stellenbosch's monuments and historic buildings are numerous bistros, coffee shops, restaurants and pubs. Among the most popular are **De Akker** – offering wine-tastings, lunch and dinner and plenty of lively regulars – and

ABOVE *Stellenbosch's farmlands brim with produce during harvest, and the Mooiberge strawberry fields are no exception.*

RIGHT *The scarecrows ward off unwanted scavengers, and help keep the Mooiberge Farmstall well stocked.*

the town of Stellenbosch, is a natural haven for the fauna and flora of the region. The wooded slopes are laced with crystal-clear streams, while nearby is the Jonkershoek Trout Hatchery, which breeds the fish for research purposes. Holders of fishing permits may also land an impressive catch here.

Situated to the southeast of Stellenbosch, and adjoining the Jonkershoek Forest and the Hottentots-Holland Nature Reserve in the Jonkershoek Valley, is **Assegaaibosch Nature Reserve**. The terrain within the reserve is covered in fynbos and is home to abundant animal life, including grysbok, duiker and mongoose; birds include black eagle and Cape sugarbird. The reserve offers short walking routes and picnic spots for visitors, and the plants in the wild flower garden are meticulously labelled and explained.

A much less strenuous way of enjoying the local flora is to make a stop at the **University of Stellenbosch Botanical Gardens** on Neethling Street. The beautiful expanse of gardens boasts both exotic and indigenous flora, succulents, lotus flowers and even bonsai trees.

For some worthwhile game viewing, try the **Wiesenhof Game Reserve** – most noted for its cheetah population – about 12 kilometres (7 miles) north of Stellenbosch. This undulating landscape of scrub and fynbos looks out over a panorama of vineyards, mountains and ocean. Facilities include a picnic and braai area, swimming pool, ice rink, coffee shop and a boating lake. Wiesenhof is closed to visitors on Mondays.

Stellenbosch on Foot

The best way to appreciate Stellenbosch's wealth of architectural treasures is to stroll its oak-shaded streets. For an unusual slant on the heritage of this university town, **Stellenbosch Historical Walks** offers daily guided walks, cultural walks, Victorian walks, ghost walks and twilight walks. Groups depart at 10am, 12.00 and 3pm weekdays or by arrangement from the Stellenbosch Tourist Bureau on Market Street. There are also tours of both the winelands and around the campus of Stellenbosch University. Inquiries: Stellenbosch Historical Walks, tel: 883-9633; Tourism and Information Centre, tel: 883-3584; Stellenbosch Tourist Bureau, tel: 883-8017.

ABOVE *The luxurious Lanzerac estate offers arguably the finest dining and accommodation in the Stellenbosch area.*

OPPOSITE *Acting as both restaurant and watering hole, De Akker is usually filled with spirited locals.*

The Wine Industry

As the heart of the country's wine and liquor industry, many of Stellenbosch's attractions centre around this enterprise. Apart from the extremely popular wine route, visitors may choose any of the guided tours and tastings offered by the cellars and distilleries based within the town itself. One such venue is the **Van Ryn Brandy Cellar** – also a popular concert venue. Tours explore the venerable art of distilling brandy, and the institute offers presentations and tours of the cellars, cooperage and distillery. Resident brandy-makers explain their craft and you may even sample – and, of course, buy – some of the liqueur brandy available. The **Oude Meester Brandy Museum** offers similar presentations but also provides some insight into the history of brandy-making and its latter-day developments.

Die Bergkelder, or 'mountain cellar', is precisely what its name suggests: a convoluted series of cellar chambers cut into the bulk of Papegaaiberg. Within the eerie cells, packed wall-to-wall with wine and lit by candles, visitors are welcome to taste the fruits of Stellenbosch's renowned vineyards.

If you intend spending a day sampling the local wines, it is recommended that you overnight in one of the many hotels and bed-and-breakfast establishments in and around Stellenbosch. Particularly popular is upmarket **Lanzerac**, lauded as one of the best hotels and restaurants in the winelands. Inevitably, your stay here will not be cheap, but the experience is unsurpassed.

USEFUL INFORMATION

Assegaaibosch Nature Reserve, tel: 887-0111
Helderberg Farm Hiking Trail, tel: 886-5858
Stellenbosch Food and Wine Festival, tel: 883-3584/883-9633.
Stellenbosch Wine Route: 36 Market St.; Mon-Fri 8.30am-1pm, 2pm-5pm; tel: 886-4310.
Tourism and Information Centre: 36 Market St.; open Mon-Fri 8am-5.30pm, Sat 9am-5pm, Sun 9.30am-4.30pm; tel: 883-3584.

PLACES OF INTEREST

Die Bergkelder: Located off Adam Tas Rd. (R44); tours Mon-Sat 10am, 10.30am and 3pm; entry fee; tel: 887-3480.
Dombeya Farm: Located near the corner of Annandale St. and Strand Rd.; open daily 9am-5pm; tel: 881-3746.
D'Ouwe Werf Country Inn: 30 Church St.; tel: 887-1608/4608.
Jean Craig Pottery: Devon Valley Rd.; open Mon-Thurs 8.15am-5pm, Fri 8.15am-4pm, Sat 9am-1pm; tel: 883-2998.
Old Lutheran Church (University of Stellenbosch Art Gallery): corner Dorp/Bird streets; open Mon-Fri 9am-5pm, Sat 9am-1pm; tel: 808-3489.
Oom Samie se Winkel: 84 Dorp St.; shop and tea garden open daily 8am-5.30pm; tel: 887-0797. Oom Samie's Fine Wine Library: 82 Dorp St.; tel: 887-2612.
Oude Libertas Centre: Adam Tas Rd. (R44); open Mon-Thurs 10am and 2.30pm, Fri 10am; tel: 808-7911. Oude Libertas Amphitheatre, tel: 808-7474.
Polkadraai Farm Stall: Polkadraai Road; tel: 881-3303.
Rembrandt van Rijn Art Museum (Libertas Parva): 31 Dorp St.; open Mon-Fri 9am-12.45pm, 2pm-5pm, Sat 10am-1pm, 2pm-5pm; tel: 886-4340.
Rhenish Complex: Bloem St.; open daily 9.30am-5pm; tel: 887-2902.
Sasol Art Museum: Eben Donges Centre, Ryneveld St.; open Mon-Fri 9am-4pm, Sat 9am-5pm, Sun 2pm-5pm; tel: 808-3695.
Stellenbosch Art Gallery: 34 Ryneveld St.; tel: 887-8343.
Stellenbosch Farmers' Winery: Adam Tas Rd. (R44); tours Mon-Thurs 10am and 2.30pm, Fri 10am; tel: 808-7569.
Stellenryck Wine Museum (Libertas Parva Cellar): Dorp St.; open Mon-Fri 9am-12.45pm, 2pm-5pm, Sat 10am-1pm, 2pm-5pm; tel: 887-3480.
Toy and Miniature Museum: cnr Market/Herte streets; open daily 9.30am-5pm; entry fee; tel: 887-2902.
University of Stellenbosch (tours), tel: 808-3211/883-3496.
University of Stellenbosch Botanical Gardens: Neethling St.; open Mon-Fri 8.30am-4.30pm, Sat 8.30am-11am; tel: 808-3054.
Van Ryn Brandy Cellar: tours Mon-Thurs 10.30am and 3pm, Fri 10.30am; tel: 881-3875.
Village Museum complex: Erfurthuis, Ryneveld St.; open Mon-Sat 9.30am-5pm, Sun 2pm-5pm; entry fee; tel: 887-2902.
Wiesenhof Game Park: off the N1 on R47; open Tues-Sun 9.30am-6pm; tel: 875-5181.

Stellenbosch
Wine Route

Excursion One

STELLENBOSCH WINE ROUTE

Stellenbosch and the surrounding vineyards are the heart of South Africa's winelands. The Stellenbosch Wine Route, with its nearly 30 estates and cellars – many granted to the original owners in the 1600s, and all within a few minutes' drive from the historic town – was opened in 1971 and ranks as one of the most popular attractions in the Western Cape. Tourists flock from all over the world to sample the fine wines and experience the rustic enchantment of the famed winelands.

Most of the estates produce excellent wines, presenting visitors with the dilemma of selecting which estates to include and which to leave off the itinerary. Although the larger wineries are certainly worth a visit, be sure to include at least one or two of the smaller estates on your tour. Also within the area are well-known wine co-operatives such as Bottelary. Beyond the strict confines of the Stellenbosch Wine Route are some fine estates, among them Zevenwacht and Thelema – especially famous for Chardonnay and Cabernet Sauvignon.

Blaauwklippen
Given to Gerrit Visser in 1692, historic **Blaauwklippen** is located on the banks of the Blaauklip River on the lower reaches of the Papagaaiberg, and is among the most picturesque of all the Cape's scenic wineries. Both the current manor house – with its typical thatch and gables and almost entirely enclosed by a traditional *stoep*, or verandah – and the adjoining Jonkershuis were erected more than 200 years ago by Dirk Hoffman. For a brief period, Blaauwklippen's vineyards were dug up and replaced by fruit orchards, and the rather dilapidated farm was purchased by Graham Boonzaier in 1971. Today the new, modern concern has regained its original stature as a winery of note – its red Zinfandel has won a number of awards. Of special interest are the new cellar – where the presses help to create the méthode champenoise Barouche sparkling wine – and the coach museum. The museum exhibits old vintners' machinery, Cape furniture and utensils, and an array of transport of yesteryear, from old Cape carts and gigs to landaus and horse-drawn omnibuses. Most are still operational and visitors may take a ride on one of these charming old conveyances. Blaauwklippen's farm shop stocks a range of country fare such as jams and chutneys. For visitors in search of a taste of the old Cape, the Coachman's lunch at the **Traditional Cape Kitchen** restaurant is a must.

PREVIOUS PAGES *With a backdrop as magnificent as the Helderberg mountains, it is little wonder that the vineyards of Stellenbosch are acclaimed among the world's most picturesque.*

INSET *Many of the vines planted in the Stellenbosch district, such as these at Delheim estate, originate from rootstock brought to the Cape from the vineyards of France.*

ABOVE *Vineyards line the roads in the Stellenbosch area.*

OPPOSITE TOP *The Lord Neethling restaurant at Neethlingshof is housed in the estate's historic homestead.*

OPPOSITE BOTTOM *Popular Delheim is one of the most visited estates on the wine route.*

Delheim

Sprawled along the slopes of Simonsberg mountain, the forerunner of present-day **Delheim** was granted to the Campher family and established as a farm in 1700. The current Delheim estate consists of three operating farms: Driesprongh and Vera Cruz – on which the wine grapes are grown – and Klapmuts. Although it produces some fine reds, the estate is most noted for its Spatzendreck Late Harvest. Another of Delheim's assets is the Vintner's Platter Restaurant which, like many of the farm restaurants in the district, concentrates on traditional Cape fare. Above Driesprongh stands the farm's cemetery, a grove of old oak trees surrounding the ruins of what was once the home of the slave who would fire the cannon from the top of Kanonkop as a signal to the farmers below that ships carrying fresh supplies were entering Table Bay.

Morgenhof

Sitting snug among the foothills of the Simonsberg lies the **Morgenhof** estate. Since its founding in 1692, Morgenhof has seen many changes, but was rescued from decline by the Momberg family, who executed an extensive reworking of the neglected land. Today, the

French-owned estate boasts an underground barrel maturation cellar topped by a French-style formal garden. Its superb wines include Chardonnay and a particularly good port. However, Morgenhof's most praised wine is its 1994 Cabernet, the estate's first release after its much-needed renovation.

Neethlingshof

First known as De Wolwedans and granted to Willem Lubbe in 1692, the 300-year-old farm on the crest of the Polkadraai on the eastern Bottelary hills became the home of colourful local character Johannes Neethling in 1816. The **Neethlingshof** estate remained the property of Neethling's descendants until 1963. The original family home has since been converted into the famed **Lord Neethling** restaurant; for simple meals, there is also the **Palm Terrace**. Top of the wine list at the Lord Neethling are the wines produced by Neethlingshof's sister cellar, **Stellenzicht**, located on the other side of the valley and unfortunately not open to the public. Neethlingshof's wines bear a distinctive label depicting the prominent avenue of pine trees for which the estate is known. The views from the farm are quite spectacular. Tours of the

cellars and vineyards – which include an excellent lunch among the vines – are exceptionally popular during the summer months, and are arranged by appointment only.

Rust-en-Vrede

The **Rust-en-Vrede** farm at the foot of the Helderberg mountains was first planted with vines in 1730, but 200 years later it no longer produced wine. Today it is the home of ex-Springbok rugby star Jannie Engelbrecht and his family, who purchased the neglected estate and replanted the vineyards. Focusing on reds, Engelbrecht continued to apply traditional vintners' techniques – including the use of French Nevere oak barrels – and produced his first wine in 1979. Both the original cellar, dating back to 1790, and the restored 1865 manor house still stand as reminders of the farm's history, but the modern cellar is a recent addition. Rust-en-Vrede's most famed products are its exceptional Cabernet, Shiraz, Tinta Barocca and Merlot.

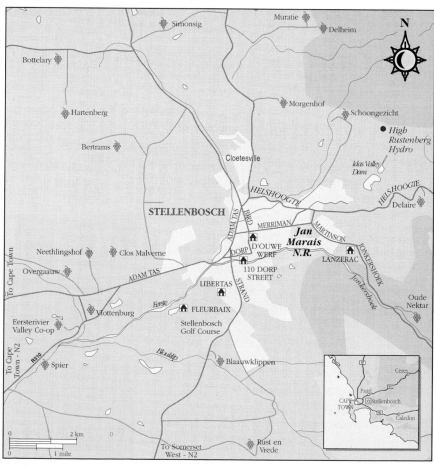

Simonsig

With its exceptional view of Simonsberg – the mountain for which the estate is named – **Simonsig** was established in 1692 and is today one of the largest private wine farms in the Cape. The estate originally comprised two farms, De Hoop and Simonsig – now amalgamated under one name and owned by the Malan family. The estate's cellars are located at De Hoop, and the Malans also lease the Kriekbult vineyards. Simonsig's first wines were released in 1968, and the Malans were the first to use the méthode champenoise to produce South African sparkling wines – supreme among them the award-winning Kaapse Vonkel. Among Simonsig's prime wines are its Gewürztraminer, Bukettraube, Chardonnay, and Pinotage and the fine 1984 Cabernet Sauvignon.

Spier

Just half an hour by road from Cape Town, the picturesque **Spier Estate** is one of the most popular stops on the Stellenbosch Wine Route. The deeds to the Spier homestead were handed to Arnout Tamboer Janz in 1692. In 1965 the estate, including five farms and fine Cape Dutch structures set amid tranquil gardens, passed into the hands of Neil Joubert, himself a descendant of wine-making Huguenots. Christian Joubert bought the first farm, Goedgekloof, in 1908 and its eighteenth-century cellars – the oldest dated cellars in South Africa – are still producing the estate's wines.

There is something for everyone here; visitors can sample the pub menu at the farm's **Taphuis**, or enjoy a light Mediterranean

Opposite Top Spier's charming old farm shop is the place to go for the estate's tempting farm produce.

Opposite Bottom The many decorative features of modern-day Neethlingshof conjure up images of its illustrious history.

Above Perfect for a leisurely picnic, the sprawling lands of Spier attract growing numbers of visitors.

USEFUL INFORMATION

The Stellenbosch Wine Route comprises the following estates and co-ops: Avontuur, Blaauwklippen, Bottelary Co-operative Winery, Clos Malverne, De Helderberg Co-operative Winery, Delaire Vineyards, Delheim, Eersterivier Valleise Co-operative Winery, Eikendal Vineyards, Hartenberg, Koopmanskloof, Lievland, Morgenhof, Muratie, Neethlingshof, Oude Nektar, Overgaauw, Rust-en-Vrede, Saxenburg Wine Farm, Simonsig, Spier, Uiterwyk, Vlottenburg Co-operative Winery, Vredenheim and Welmoed Co-operative Wine Cellars.

Blaauwklippen: sales/tasting open Mon-Fri 9am-5pm, Sat 9am-1pm; cellar tours Mon-Fri 11am & 3pm, Sat 11am; Traditional Cape Kitchen restaurant (lunch), open Mon-Sat 12pm-2pm (1 Oct-30 Apr); tel: 880-0133/4.

Delheim: sales/tasting open Mon-Fri 8.30am-5pm, Sat 9am-3pm, Sun 11.30am-3pm (Nov-Feb); cellar tours Mon-Fri 10.30am & 2pm (1 Oct-30 Apr), Sat 10.30am (all year); tel: 882-2036; Vintner's Platter Restaurant open Mon-Sat 12pm-2pm, Sun 12pm-2.30pm (Nov-Feb); tel: 882-2297.

Morgenhof: sales/tasting open daily; light lunches served daily; tel: 889-5510; e-mail: morgenhof@iafrica.com

Neethlingshof: sales/tasting open Mon-Fri 9am-5pm, Sat-Sun 10am-4pm; no restaurant; tel: 883-8988; Palm Terrace and The Lord Neethling restaurants, tel: 883-8966.

Rust-en-Vrede: sales/tasting open Mon-Fri 8.30am-5pm, Sat 9.30am-1pm; no restaurant; tel: 881-3000.

Simonsig: sales and tasting open Mon-Fri 8.30am-5pm, Sat 8.30am-4.30pm; cellar tours Mon-Fri 10am & 3pm, Sat 10am; no restaurant; tel: 882-2044.

Spier: sales open 9am-5pm daily; tasting open daily 10am-4pm (on the hour); cellar tours 12pm & 3pm (booking essential); Café Spier open 9am-5pm (November-May); Jonkershuis Restaurant open daily 12pm-5pm (lunch), Fri-Sat 6.30pm-11pm (dinner); Taphuis tavern open daily 9am-11pm; tel: 881-3096.

Wineland Ballooning, tel: 863-3192.

---

lunch at the graceful **Café Spier**. For more hearty, traditional meals, try the renowned Jonkershuis Restaurant, while the **Spier Wine Centre** caters for wine lovers. The open-air amphitheatre, with live performances of classical, jazz and popular music, attracts enthusiastic crowds. Concerts are particularly enjoyable with either a pre-packed picnic lunch sold by the estate kitchens, or one crammed with goodies – bread, baguettes, preserves and fresh produce – bought from the Spier farmstall. The setting is quite enchanting, and country attractions include wine-tastings, the **Cheetah Park** (benefiting the Cheetah Conservation Fund), pony trips or rides on the old horse-drawn carts from the Equestrian Centre. The elegant Opstal manor house may be hired for private functions.

Paarl

Excursion Two

$\mathscr{P}$AARL

$\mathscr{T}$he first records of what was to become the town of Paarl date from 1668, just six years after Jan van Riebeeck landed in Table Bay. The first farmers would settle along the banks of the Berg River some 30 years later. In the more than 300 years since these tentative explorations, Paarl has become not only one of the country's main wine-producing areas, but a seat of South African culture and hospitality.

Paarl's name comes from the pearl-like granite mountain – one of the world's largest exposed granite domes – which rises above the town. Views from here take in the valley of the Berg River (on which the annual canoe marathon is held in July) and, in the distance, Table Mountain and the Atlantic Ocean. Paarl is filled with history yet offers the finest in contemporary dining as well as the lure of the surrounding wine estates.

Historic Town

The architecture of Paarl is quite exceptional, and the Paarl Museum arranges special tours which walk visitors through the most impressive examples, including Georgian, Edwardian and Cape Dutch homes. Included on the tour are the charming old thatched Strooidakkerk and Zeederberg Square on Main Street. The **Paarl Museum** is located in the Oude Pastorie, the original village parsonage on Main Street, and houses contemporary and old Cape artefacts such as furniture, silverware and household goods of the colonial era. The magnificent 18th-century gabled mansion offers fascinating insights into early colonial life.

La Concorde, on Main Street in South Paarl, is the headquarters of the KWV, the primary exporter of South African wines. However, the KWV Wingerdspens on Kohler Street just behind the offices is where the co-operative winemakers association offers sales and tastings, and hosts cellar tours and lectures where visitors may learn about the creation and appreciation of local wines. It is here, too, that visitors can buy barrels and other wine-making curios and, of course, cases of KWV's popular fortified wines. The company's **Cathedral Cellar** houses the world's largest wine vats.

In the early days of the Cape colony, wagons were the primary mode of transport and Paarl was the last stop for wagons venturing into the hinterland. The **Paarl Wagonmakers Museum** tells the fascinating story of this important local

---

PREVIOUS PAGES *Bountiful flora garlands the scenic Paarl Mountain Nature Reserve.*

INSET *The gabled, Dutch-style Oude Pastorie in Main Street houses the fascinating Paarl Museum.*

ABOVE *Waterblommetjies ('water flowers') plucked from the water at Schoongezicht are used to make a rich traditional Cape stew.*

OPPOSITE TOP *The common swallowtail butterfly is among the many butterfly species to be seen at Butterfly World near Klapmuts.*

OPPOSITE BOTTOM LEFT *In typical rural style, pumpkins are dried on the rooftops of even a quaint local coffee shop.*

OPPOSITE BOTTOM RIGHT *Many of Paarl's modern businesses have made their homes in the restored homes of yesteryear.*

industry. Exhibits include all sorts of implements and tools used in the manufacture of the all-important wagons.

For more contemporary handmade goods, visit **Le Cott Gifts and Decor**, where you can buy household novelties such as meticulously handpainted cloths and the like. Fresh local farm produce may be found at both the **Onverwacht Kontreiwinkel** on the outskirts of town and **Bien Donné Fruit Farm**, which boasts a herb garden, farmstall and intimate restaurant.

However, for connoisseurs of country life, an evening at **Bosman's Restaurant** will surpass all expectations. Located in a traditional Cape Dutch home at the **Grande Roche Hotel** on the corner of Plantasie and Constantia roads in the middle of Paarl, Bosman's is considered by many to be the finest restaurant – at the finest hotel – in the Cape. The food and hospitality are outstanding, and the impressive wine reflects the richness of the surrounding winelands.

Paarl is also noted for high-quality handicrafts. Foremost among local crafters is **Clementina van der Walt**, the talented and highly respected ceramic artist whose famous studios are situated in Langenhoven Street. Visitors may browse through the exquisite pottery and tableware available direct to the public. Another famed crafts centre is the **Ikhweze Centre**, where the weavers of Bhabhathane (Xhosa for 'butterfly' and symbolizing the rich colour for which they are noted) use karakul wool and mohair to fashion traditional garments, tapestries and rugs by hand. The centre also displays and sells the work of artists from Mbekweni, a small town located on the way to Wellington. For those visitors who delight in handmade items, be sure to spend a Saturday morning at the Paarl flea market, or drop by the Art and Craft Market in Victoria Park, held on the first Saturday of every month.

Wildlife

The most popular place to view the region's wildlife at close range is the **Le Bonheur Crocodile Farm**, on the Babylonstoren Road just beyond the town limits. A network of footpaths run between dams which hold more than 1 000 of these prehistoric-looking reptiles, ranging from young adults of about a metre long to giants of up to five metres (15 feet) in length. The farm's breeding programme allows for the harvesting of crocodile skins, which are used to produce fine leather products ranging from small souvenirs to quality shoes and handbags. The farm also has its own restaurant and tour facilities. At the nearby **Die Vonds Snake Centre**, the reptiles are somewhat smaller but no less fascinating.

The bird sanctuary that stretches along the banks of the Berg River is an ideal destination for bird-watchers. The tranquil sanctuary boasts more than 130 species, including eagles, and water birds such as flamingos, maccoa ducks and the beautiful malachite kingfisher.

Ostriches are equally common in the Paarl area and at least two local ostrich farms have opened their doors to the public. Both **Heen en Weer Ostrich Farm** and the **Wine Route Ostrich Farm** offer tours, a gift shop selling indigenous crafts and curios, and speciality restaurants with menus that feature tender cuts of ostrich meat.

Be sure to take time to stop at **Butterfly World** at Klapmuts, where magnificent wild specimens flit among the lush vegetation in the natural surrounds. This is a particularly exciting excursion for young children and nature lovers.

Millwater Flower Garden, which is enveloped in the colourful blooms of succulents, vygies and azanias during the spring months – be sure to catch the Chrysanthemum Show in May. Facilities within the reserve include picnic and braai areas, and the dams offer opportunities for fishing – black bass is especially plentiful.

The **Paarl Mountain Nature Reserve** has numerous walks and trails varying from the strenuous to the casual stroll. Virtually in the middle of town, however, is the **Arboretum**, a green oasis watered by the Berg River and containing more than 700 species of flora.

The Paarl Wine Route

Although not quite as popular as the more famous Stellenbosch Wine Route, the Paarl route is extraordinarily beautiful, and the vineyards of the Berg River Valley produce some excellent wines. The lush countryside is virtually covered with vines, and the 17 estates on the official Paarl Wine Route (which includes the farms around the neighbouring town of Wellington) make for a relaxing and memorable tour. As well as the world-renowned KWV, the Paarl area is home to the Stellenbosch Farmers' Winery's famous **Nederburg** estate, the venue for a noted annual wine auction.

In celebration of the district's wine-making heritage, the first Saturday in April is dedicated to the annual Paarl Nouveau Wine Festival, and the first weekend in September to the Sparkling Wine Festival. Selecting which estates you will visit is an unenviable task, but be sure to taste the products of a variety of wine-makers rather than linger at just one or two farms.

Backsberg

Heralded as one of the country's finest wine producers, the **Backsberg** estate is situated on the Simonsberg. The farm was not originally planted with vines, but when Lithuanian

Paarl Mountain

Undoubtedly the most noticeable landmark on the slopes of Paarlberg is the **Taal Monument**, a trio of tall structures pointing towards the skies. These commemorate the three elements that contributed to the development of the Afrikaans language: the civilisation of Europe, the heritage of slaves from the East and the influence of the African continent. The site also includes an amphitheatre, which serves as an entertainment venue, and picnic spots from which to admire the magnificent view over the surrounding countryside. The **Afrikaans Language Museum** is situated in Pastorie Street in the town itself, and prides itself on exhibitions which not only look at the history of Afrikaner culture but also on the many activities and projects revolving around Afrikaans in the modern era.

Overlooking the wide Groot Drakenstein valley is the **Paarl Mountain Nature Reserve**, an expanse of wild country resting uniquely on granite clay. The veld is covered with wild flowers, rare species of indigenous fynbos vegetation, floral gems such as orchids, and natural forest glades. The pastoral environment is ideal for hiking and climbing and there are a number of demarcated walking and driving routes – such as the Jan Phillips Mountain Drive – through some of the most inspiring vistas in the Western Cape. One of the prime attractions is the

---

ABOVE *The 300-year-old town of Paarl is watched over by the glittering monolith of pearl-like Paarl Rock.*

RIGHT *The dimly-lit cellars of the Backsberg estate occupy a cave carved out of the local rock.*

OPPOSITE *The milk of Fairview's agile Swiss goats, at home on their manmade 'mountainside', is used to make fine cheese.*

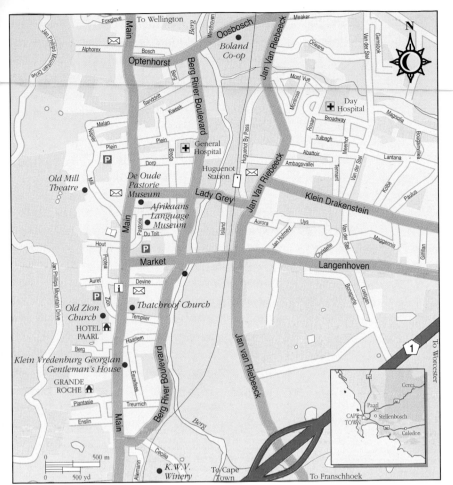

and is credited with introducing a fortified sweet shiraz and being the first to make Gamay Nouveau using a unique carbonic maceration method. In 1990 Fairview also introduced a sparkling wine pressed in the méthode champenoise from Pinot Noir grapes. The almost purple Zinfandel produced by the estate is also quite exceptional, with an alcohol content of 16.5 per cent.

As recently as 1981, Fairview imported Saanen goats from Switzerland and entered the cheese market, producing feta, pecorino and other cheeses. The Swiss mountain goats are a popular attraction on the farm, and may be seen making their nimble way up and down the specially built staircase to their loft home. They have since been joined by milk-producing sheep imported from Germany to make the estate's Portuguese Cesa de Serra, or 'cheese of the mountains.'

Laborie

A 19th-century Cape Dutch homestead on Taillefert Street in Paarl, **Laborie** is owned by the KWV, who transformed the estate from a fruit and table grape farm to the reputable wine estate of today. The official name of the range is now Laborie Taillefert after its founder, Jean Taillefert,

immigrant Charles Back bought the land in 1916, he set about establishing a wine estate. In 1938, he was joined by his son Sydney, the current proprietor of the farm. The Backs concentrated on fine reds, but Sydney Back is acclaimed as being the first South African producer to plant chardonnay grapes. Today Backsberg also produces oak-matured brandy, but wines remain the most successful export. The estate has grown considerably, so that today it is a fine establishment with its own wine museum and tours – the atmospheric cave cellar is particularly impressive – which are enhanced by state-of-the-art audio-visual equipment.

Fairview

Known for its quality wines, **Fairview** has also become famous for its cheeses. The farm on the southern stretch of Paarl Mountain was bought in 1937 by Charles Back (of Backsberg fame), and is today run by a second son, Cyril, whose own son Charles is the cellarmaster. After the death of his father, Cyril concentrated on quality red wines and his dry red Cinsaut is very highly acclaimed, having won a number of coveted awards. The young Charles Back has continued in the family tradition,

and commemorates the arrival at the Cape of the first French Huguenots in 1688. Facilities at Laborie include a wine-tasting centre (converted from the original cellar), its own traditional Cape restaurant and Wine House. Tastings and tours, however, are by arrangement only.

Nederburg

Established more than two centuries ago, **Nederburg** has become synonymous with fine wines – with more than 1 000 awards to its credit – and is particularly renowned for its world-famous wine auction held annually in March. Situated in the Klein Drakenstein, the historic Cape Dutch manor was erected in 1800 by Phillipus Wolvaard. When German-born Johann Graue bought the farm in 1937, he planted the exceptional vineyards that Nederburg boasts today. With his son Arnold, Graue also perfected a unique process whereby cold water is used to slow down the fermentation that the high temperatures common during harvest would normally accelerate. Sadly, Arnold Graue died in 1953 – a year after walking away with numerous awards at the Cape Wine Show. Today, the famed estate continues to produce some exceptional wines, among them the celebrated dessert wine, Edelkeur.

Rhebokskloof

The setting of **Rhebokskloof** is like something out of a grand historical novel. Based in the original Cape Dutch structures erected in 1692 and surrounded by a picture-book countryside, Rhebokskloof is rural living at its best. The paddocks hold horses, and Ile-de-France sheep are kept for stud purposes, while the antelope after which the estate is named wander among the hills, black eagles wing overhead and black swans glide on the farm dams. Visitors looking for fine food should not miss the estate's restaurant, as well as the convivial outdoor eatery with splendid views over the vineyards.

Simonsvlei Co-op

In comparison to the major wineries in the district, the **Simonsvlei** wine co-operative was established relatively recently – in 1945 – and today it is instantly recognisable by the giant wine bottle standing at the entrance to its cellar.

Simonsvlei's enormous variety of wines is due largely to the wide area it covers. As a co-operative – the first to be represented at the Nederburg Auction – the winemakers here use grapes from the Klein Drakenstein, Wemmershoek, Paarlberg, Simonsberg and Muldersvlei and elsewhere to create the fine wines for which Simonsvlei has become known. One of its most distinctive creations is the award-winning 1973 Cabernet Sauvignon, still much sought after. The facilities here include an impressive, modern visitors' centre, opened to the

public in 1989. Included on the estate is a restaurant; don't miss the summer lunch in the gardens of the cellar, and tasting and cellar tours to match the best. Booking is essential and tours depend largely on the season.

Zandwijk Wine Farm

Established in 1689 by Willem van Wyk, the picturesque Zandwijk Farm on the slopes of Paarl Mountain was somewhat dilapidated when Jacobus Bosman purchased the land in 1742 and began to plant vineyards. However, by the time the current owners, Cape Gate – a group of Johannesburg entrepreneurs – bought the farm, it had slipped into decline and was barely viable. The businessmen immediately set to prepare the vines for wine-making and to restore the farm's grand old homestead, which dates back to 1785. Today, **Zandwijk** is the only wine estate in the country which boasts a kosher wine list. Vintner Leon Mostert, under the supervision of the Beth Din, travelled to Israel to study the wine-making process there; today, all the additives in the production of Zandwijk's wines are strictly kosher. The cellars are open by appointment but are closed on the Jewish Sabbath.

OPPOSITE TOP *The vineyards of Paarl produce some of the finest wine grapes in the country.*

OPPOSITE BOTTOM *From the farmlands of Laborie estate, visitors glimpse the Afrikaans Taal Monument's towering spires.*

ABOVE *Paarl is the headquarters of the KWV, one of the giants of the South African wine industry.*

Paarl Publicity Association: 216 Main St., corner Main/Auret; open Mon-Fri 9am-5pm, Sat 9am-1pm, Sun 10am-1pm; tel: 872-3829/4842.

PLACES OF INTEREST

Afrikaans Language Museum: 11 Pastorie Rd.; open Mon-Fri 8am-5pm; tel: 872-3441.
Butterfly World: Klapmuts; open daily 9am-5pm; tel: 875-5628.
Clementina Ceramic Studio: on the R303; open Mon-Fri 9am-5pm, Sat 9am-2pm, Sun 10am-1pm; tel: 872-3420.
Die Vonds Snake Centre: open Mon-Fri 9am-5pm, Sat 9am-2pm, Sun 10am-1pm; tel: 863-8309.
Die Wingerdspens: Kohler Rd.; open Mon-Fri 9am-5pm, Sat 9am-2pm, Sun 10am-1pm; tel: 863-3803.
Heen en Weer Ostrich Farm: on the R44; open Mon-Fri 9am-5pm, Sat 9am-2pm, Sun 10am-1pm; tel: 875-5393.
Grande Roche Hotel: corner Plantasie/Constantia roads; tel: 863-2727.
KWV: Main St.; sales/tastings open Mon-Fri 8am-4pm, Sat 8.30am-4pm, Sun 10am-2.30pm; cellar tours by appointment; tel: 807-3007/8.
Le Bonheur Crocodile Farm: Babylonstoren Rd.; open daily 9.30am-5pm; entry fee; tel: 863-1142.
Onverwacht Kontreiwinkel: on the R44, 13km off the N1; open Mon-Fri 9am-5pm, Sat 9am-2pm, Sun 10am-1pm; tel: 863-8123.
Paarl Museum: 303 Main St.; open Mon-Fri 10am-5pm, Sat 10am-4pm, Sun 2.30pm-5pm; admission by donation; tel: 872-2651.
Wine Route Ostrich Farm: on the R44; open Mon-Fri 9am-5pm, Sat 9am-2pm, Sun 10am-1pm; tel: 872-6023.

THE PAARL WINE ROUTE

Estates on the Paarl (and Wellington*) wine routes include Backsberg, Belcher, Bolandse*, Bovlei, Fairview, Laborie, Landskroon, Nederburg, Onverwacht*, Rhebokskloof, Simondium, Simonsvlei, Villiera, Wamakersvallei*, Wellington Co-op*, Windmeul and Zandwijk. For information on the **Paarl Wine Route:** tel: 872-3605.
Backsberg: sales/tasting open Mon-Fri 8.30am-5pm, Sat 8.30am-1pm; cellar tours; tel: 875-5141.
Fairview: wine and cheese sales/tasting open Mon-Fri 8am-5.30pm, Sat 8am-1pm; no cellar tours; no restaurant; tel: 863-2450.
Laborie: Taillefert St.; sales/tasting open Mon-Fri 9am-5pm, Sat 9am-1pm; tel: 807-3390; Laborie Restaurant & Wine House, tel: 807-3095.
Nederburg: sales/tasting open Mon-Fri 8.30am-5pm, Sat 9am-1pm; cellar tours by appointment; no restaurant; tel: 862-3104.
Rhebokskloof: sales/tasting open Feb-Nov Mon-Sun 9am-5pm; Dec-Jan Mon/Thurs/Fri/Sat 9am-7.30pm, Tues/Wed/Sun 9am-5pm; tel: 863-8386; cellar tours by appointment; restaurant open Mon-Sun lunch, Wed/Fri/Sat dinner; tel: 863-8606.
Simonsvlei Co-op: sales/tasting open Mon-Fri 8am-5pm, Sat 8.30am-4.30pm; seasonal cellar tours; restaurant; tel: 863-3040.
Zandwijk Wine Farm: sales/tasting Mon-Fri 8am-12.30pm, 1.30pm-5pm; cellar tours by appointment; tel: 863-2368/70.

Franschhoek

Excursion Three

FRANSCHHOEK

The tranquil valley cradling the town of Franschhoek is one of the country's most awe-inspiring landscapes, and one of its most prolific wine-producing areas. The town's name means 'French Corner', in reference to the 200 Huguenot families who fled persecution in France to settle amid the Cape mountains in 1688. They brought with them the culture and sophistication of their native land, as well as superb wine-making skills. Although the Huguenots were soon assimilated into the local culture, Franschhoek's French heritage is still discernible, especially in the fine cuisine for which the area is renowned. In April every year the town celebrates its French origins with the Franschhoek Festival, but visitors throughout the year will delight in the multitude of art galleries, antique shops and craft outlets which line its quaint streets.

Most visitors arrive in Franschhoek via the road from Stellenbosch. The other access route to the town is from the southeast via the picturesque **Franschhoek Pass**, and across the original bridge built by Jan Joubert in 1823. This is one of the oldest bridges still in use in South Africa, and offers sensational views over the valley.

Franschhoek's greatest attraction is the many restaurants and bistros, most of which are distinctly French in style and origin. The town boasts the largest number of award-winning restaurants in the country, and menus vary from French provincial to Cape Malay. Some of the finest establishments include **Le Quartier Français** (French food at its best), **La Petite Ferme** (country hospitality with dramatic views), **La Maison de Chamonix** (known for its Sunday buffet and picnics) and **Chez Michel** (continental dishes in a relaxed bistro setting). Most of these restaurants are within the town itself, and – unlike other wineland areas – few are located on the surrounding estates.

The Town

The most recognisable landmark in the town is the **Huguenot Memorial Museum** and **Huguenot Monument** on Lambrecht Street, which commemorates the arrival of the French immigrants more than 250 years ago. The Huguenot Monument took 10 years to complete and was finally opened in 1948 as a symbol of the religious freedom enjoyed by the French here. The arches of the monument symbolise the Holy

---

PREVIOUS PAGES *The picnic lawns of Boschendal are blessed with towering trees, a tranquil pond and fairytale gazebo.*

PREVIOUS PAGE INSET *Come summer, the grape harvest heralds the arrival of another memorable vintage.*

ABOVE *Forever a symbol of liberty, the Huguenot Monument remains as testimony to the town's rich French heritage.*

OPPOSITE TOP *As the home of some of the country's finest cuisine, Franschhoek boasts a multitude of restaurants and bistros.*

OPPOSITE BOTTOM LEFT *The Huguenot Memorial Museum occupies a stately house that was moved here from Cape Town.*

OPPOSITE BOTTOM RIGHT *Central to the Huguenot Monument is a figure of a woman casting off the cloak of oppression.*

Trinity, while the woman carrying a Bible and a broken chain represents freedom of religion, and rejects oppression by casting off her cloak. The fleur-de-lys design on her garments reflects nobility and the globe beneath her feet symbolises freedom of spirit. The Huguenot Museum also operates as a research centre, providing information and genealogical data on the French families who settled here.

On Dirkie Uys Street is the **La Cotte Watermill**, restored to its 1779 glory with funds from the Franschhoek Vineyards Co-operative located on Main Street. Tours of the mill are by prior arrangement, but it is worth the effort to see this fascinating piece of history. Not far away is the **La Cotte Inn**, on the corner of Louis Botha and Huguenot streets, where visitors can sample and buy the wines produced in the Franschhoek Valley.

The town is also home to a number of crafts and home industries, including **Kei Carpets**. To see examples of local art, visit the gallery on Bordeaux Street. For those with a keen interest in flora, a stop at the Bonne Valeur Rose Farm is a must.

Mont Rochelle Nature Reserve

In close proximity to both the Hawequas and Nuweberg state forests, the 1 760 hectares (4 349 acres) of the **Mont Rochelle Nature Reserve** are unspoilt and quite breathtaking, and ideal territory for walking and hiking. Trails within the reserve offer some scenic routes, and equally impressive is the two- to three-day Boland Hiking Trail, but permission to go on this trail must be obtained from the local municipality, the Franschhoek Museum or the Franschhoek Valley tourism office. Consisting largely of natural fynbos, the area covers the tracks and paths originally made by migrating wildlife – including elephants – and these very access routes were later followed by the European settlers in order to cross the rugged

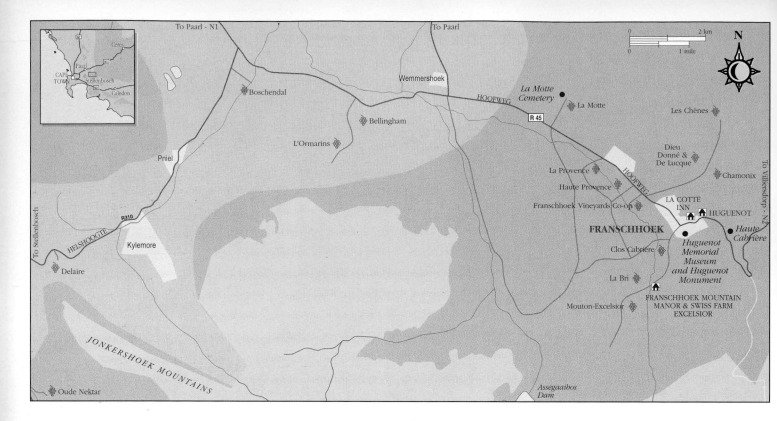

mountain ranges. Although open to visitors throughout the year, Mont Rochelle remains much as it was during these pioneering days and there are no recreation facilities or accommodation within the reserve. Visitors will, however, be treated to sightings of indigenous flora and fauna, among them baboon, rhebok, grysbok, klipspringer, about 30 species of reptile and the ever-present dassies.

The Franschhoek Wine Route

Established to commemorate the Huguenots and the founding vintners of the area's winelands, the **Franschhoek Wine Route** – also known as the Vignerons de Franschhoek – comprises 16 of South Africa's most distinguished wine-makers.

Estates along the scenic route include Bellingham, Boschendal, Chamonix, Clos Cabrière, Haute Provence, La Bri, La Motte, La Provence and L'Ormarins, all of which trace their origins to the Gallic settlers. However, because the vast majority of Franschhoek wines originate at the co-operative, there are few cellar tours. All are conveniently located at the Franschhoek Wine Co-operative and cellars on Main Street.

Bellingham

Nestled at the base of the Groot Drakenstein Mountains, the original land was first owned by Gerrit Jansze van Vuuren – granted in 1693 – but gradually fell into disrepair. The **Bellingham** estate was finally bought and upgraded by the Podlashuks family in 1943, who planted the farm's very first vines. The estate soon developed into one of the most successful in the Franschhoek Valley, and its wines were much sought after both locally and abroad – Bellingham wines were even served on the Union-Castle passenger liners travelling between Cape Town and the United Kingdom.

LEFT *Remnants of a bygone era are plentiful in Franschhoek, and merge well with the modern town.*

OPPOSITE TOP *Boschendal's renovated Cape-Flemish homestead is a tribute to the rich heritage of the region.*

OPPOSITE BOTTOM *Exhibits at the Franschhoek Museum date back to the early days of the wine industry.*

The farm was bought by Union Wine Ltd in 1970 – a modern cellar and visitors' centre was opened in 1985 – and then purchased by Kangra Holdings under Graham Beck. In 1991 Beck amalgamated with Kersaf – under the auspices of hotel king Sol Kerzner – to form Douglas Green Bellingham.

Boschendal

The **Boschendal** estate was granted to Frenchman Jean le Long who, in turn, sold the property to fellow countryman Abraham de Villiers 30 years later. An expert vintner with a number of recommendations to his credit, De Villiers had arrived at the Cape in 1689 and was to become one of the settlement's most prominent and respected winemakers. The family name is still highly regarded within the region's winelands, and Boschendal was one of the few estates to remain with only one owner for more than 160 years. Following the devastation of the vines by disease, the De Villiers family was compelled to sell the land in 1879 to the alternative crop farming project initiated by Cecil John Rhodes. Because fruit was less susceptible to the dangers of disease, Rhodes Fruit Farms concentrated on more varied fruit farming and began exporting the new crops to the United Kingdom. The property was finally procured by the Anglo American Corporation in 1969. Under the guidance of architect Gabriel Fagan, the new proprietors restored both the farm and Cape-Flemish homestead erected by De Villiers in 1812.

The original buildings of Boschendal today house the modern developments of the estate. While the main house is the centre of the wine operation, the old Waenhuis – or wagon house – now serves as the gift and curio shop. Still standing is the Taphuis, the farm's oldest building, but a new modern winery has recently been added. Boschendal offers cellar tours, tastings and opportunities for buying wines, as well as a range of good eating venues. Not only is there a table d'hôte restaurant and light meals served by the popular Le Café, but the estate's Le Pique Nique sells packed picnic lunches during the summer months which may be enjoyed on the lawns shaded by oak trees and umbrellas.

Chamonix

Once part of the La Cotte wine estate – one of the first to be granted to Huguenots in 1688 – the land was originally known as Waterval, but as **Chamonix** has come to symbolize the best of Franschhoek. The Malan family, who took over the farm in 1947, began establishing the lands for quality grapes, and when the Pickering family purchased the property in 1965, they introduced other fruit and timber. Today, the estate – set high up in the valley and boasting its own restaurant and guest accommodation – consistently produces excellent wine grapes. Its wines are created in the cellars of the Franschhoek Vineyards Co-operative. Chamonix produced its first wines in 1983 – initially only Vin Blanc and Blanc de Rouge (now known as Blanc de Noir) – and then, in 1985, its famed Rhine Riesling. All its wines – uniquely bottled in claret bottles – may be bought and tasted on site, but visitors must make an appointment to tour the cellars.

Clos Cabrière

Cradled by mountains, this beautiful estate makes the most of its exceptional setting, carefully orchestrating the elements of sun, soil and vine to create great wines. Founded in 1694 by Pierre Jourdan and named after his home town, Cabrière estate has seen many owners make many changes to the lands. The relatively small farm currently known as **Clos Cabrière**, forming only a portion of Jourdan's original estate, is the property of flamboyant Achim von Arnim, the highly acclaimed wine-maker at Boschendal, whose own interests lie largely in the méthode champenoise, by which he creates his excellent sparkling wines, using only chardonnay and pinot noir grapes. Conditions at Clos Cabrière are ideal for this type of wine, and Von Arnim has enjoyed much success with many of his wines (and those he has created for Boschendal), commanding good prices and even higher acclaim.

Franschhoek Vineyards Co-operative

The winery, founded in 1945 by Alberto Agostini, is based on the old La Cotte farmstead. Known for his innovative cellar methods, Agostini laid the groundwork for a fine winery. Today, however, it is home to a wine co-operative to which members contribute their grape harvest in order to produce wines. La Cotte sells wines under its own label, and about six of the 123 members have their own wines bottled here rather than produced under the collective name. The rest of the grapes are used to create wines which are sold to wholesalers. The co-operative offers both tastings and sales.

La Motte

Nearly 300 years old, **La Motte** was originally the property of Pierre Joubert, but it was sold a number of times after his death until acquired by vintner Gabriel du Toit. In an ironic twist of fate, Gideon Joubert, great-grandson of Pierre, bought the farm in 1915. In commemoration of his ancestor, Joubert re-established the farmlands as vineyards and renovated the mansion, presiding over the rejuvenated La Motte for more than 40 years. The farm was bought by the renowned Rupert family in 1970 who, in turn, restored the main house and outbuildings. The original cellar was modified to accommodate the maturation processes, and a modern cellar was opened in 1985. Although there are no tours of the cellars, it is open for wine sales and tasting. The first wines produced here were L'Etoile Légère (a low-alcohol Sauvignon Blanc) and a Blanc de Noir. The latter was created using both Shiraz and Cabernet Sauvignon.

L'Ormarins

Dating back to 1694, when it was granted to Jean Roi, **L'Ormarins** is probably one of the most beautiful estates in the Franschhoek Valley. The gabled splendour of the homestead built by later owners, the De Villiers family, looks out over a magnificent man-made lake, and the T-shaped house that is currently home to the estate manager is the oldest structure on the farm. The original 1799 wine cellar, complete with casks engraved with the coats of arms of Huguenot settlers, is now used as a store. One of the first signs of its success dates back to the 19th century when owner Izaak Marais was acclaimed for his 1833 Cape Madeira. Now owned by Antonij Rupert who bought it from his father, Anton, L'Ormarins is renowned both for its reds – among them Cabernet Sauvignon, Merlot, and Shiraz – and white wines – Sauvignon Blanc, Weisser and Cape Riesling, Chenin Blanc and Chardonnay – all of which are bottled at Bergkelder. L'Ormarins offers neither a restaurant nor tours of its cellars, but the public is welcome to taste its wines.

OPPOSITE TOP *The views of the Franschhoek Valley from the Franschhoek Pass are unsurpassed.*

OPPOSITE BOTTOM *The Franschhoek Vineyards Co-operative offers a range of facilities and expertise to the region's farmers.*

ABOVE *The atmospheric tasting room of L'Ormarins invites visitors to sample its celebrated wines.*

Boland Hiking Trail: tel 886-5858.
Franschhoek Vallée Tourism: 2 Main St., PO Box 178, Franschhoek 7690; tel/fax: 876-3603.

PLACES OF INTEREST
Bonne Valeur Rose Farm: Daniel Hugo Rd.; open Mon-Sat 9am-5pm, Sun 2pm-5pm; tel: 876-2228.
Bordeaux Street Gallery: Bordeaux St.; open Mon-Fri 9am-5pm, Sat 9am-1pm, Sun 2pm-5pm; tel: 876-2165.
Huguenot Memorial Museum: Lambrecht St.; open Mon-Fri 9am-5pm, Sat 9am-1pm, 2pm-5pm, Sun 2pm-5pm; entry fee; tel: 876-2532.
Kei Carpets: Main St.; open Mon-Fri 9am-5pm, Sat 9am-1pm; tel: 876-2192.
La Cotte Inn: corner Louis Botha/Huguenot streets; open daily; tel: 876-3775.
Mont Rochelle Nature Reserve: open daily 8.30am-5pm; tel: 876-3000.
Vignerons de Franschhoek Tasting Centre: tel: 876-3062.

RESTAURANTS
Brinjals, tel: 876-2151.
Chez Michel, tel: 876-2671.
Haute Cabrière Cellar, tel: 876-3688; e-mail: cabriere@iafrica.com.
La Cotte, tel: 876-2081.
La Maison de Chamonix, tel: 876-2393.
La Petite Ferme, tel: 876-3016.
Le Ballon Rouge, tel: 876-2651.
Le Quartier Français, tel: 876-2151.

THE FRANSCHHOEK WINE ROUTE
Estates on the Franschhoek Wine Route include: Bellingham, Boschendal, Chamonix, Clos Cabrière, Dieu Donné, Franschhoek Vineyards Co-operative, Haute Provence, La Bourgogne, La Bri, La Motte, La Provence, L'Ormarins, Mont Rochelle, Môreson Blois, Mouton-Excelsior.
Bellingham: sales/tasting open Mon-Fri 8.30am-4.30pm, Sat 10am-12pm; tel: 874-1011.
Boschendal: sales/tasting open Mon-Fri 8.30am-4.30pm, Sat 8.30am-12.30pm, Dec-Jan: Mon-Fri 8.30am-4.30pm, Sat 8.30am-4.30pm, Sun: 8.30-12.30; cellar tours; Le Café restaurant; table d'hôte restaurant; Le Pique Nique (picnic baskets) Nov-Apr; tel 874-1031.
Chamonix: sales/tasting open daily 9.30am-4pm; cellar tours by appointment; restaurant and accommodation; tel: 876-2498/2494.
Franschhoek Vineyards Co-operative: sales and tasting open Mon-Fri 9am-1pm, 2pm-4.30pm, Sat 10am-1pm; tel: 876-2086.
La Motte: sales/tasting open Mon-Fri 9am-4pm, Sat 9am-12pm; no restaurant; no cellar tours; tel: 876-3119.
L'Ormarins: sales/tasting open Mon-Fri 9am-4.30pm, Sat 9am-12pm; no restaurant; no cellar tours; tel: 876-3119.
La Provence: Main Road (R45); tel: 876-2616.

West Coast &
Namaqualand

Excursion Four

WEST COAST & NAMAQUALAND

The rugged beauty of the West Coast and Namaqualand make these regions tempting destinations for any visitor to the Cape. The West Coast extends from the suburb of Milnerton, just beyond the northern reaches of the peninsula, to the village of Velddrif, and is undoubtedly one of the country's most inspiring stretches of shoreline. The simple landscape of gentle fynbos and endless beach looks out over the waters of the Atlantic Ocean, and combines an uncomplicated lifestyle with a wealth of wildlife. But the most popular of its abundant attractions must be its spring wild flowers. Further north, the harsh beauty of Namaqualand's semi-arid wilderness is softened annually by this same miraculous abundance of spring wild flowers.

The West Coast forms part of what is known as the Cape Floral Kingdom, a unique biome which incorporates more than 1 000 flowering species, with no less than 80 plants specific to this corner of the world. Although plants vary from tubers and bulbs to legumes and herbal varieties such as buchu, the area may be divided into sandveld, renosterveld and fynbos. The most prolific vegetation type is the shrub-like fynbos, which comprises delicate ericas, reed-like restios and grand proteas. It is, however, the magnificent array of colour of the daisies, mesembryanthemums and other annuals that attracts so many visitors to the West Coast and Namaqualand every year. To keep abreast of where the finest displays are to be found, visitors can telephone the **Flowerline** service. Generally, the parade of flowers is best viewed from August to mid-October, and is at its finest at around midday. Visitors should note that in order to appreciate the full glory, be sure to view with the sun at your back – the flowers tend to face the rays of the sun and if you're at their back chances are you will see very little colour at all. Both for conservation purposes and for the enjoyment of other visitors, the flowers may not be picked.

Of course, an added attraction to the area is its prolific birdlife, which lures birders from all over the country. Naturally, the most common species are the water birds, such as gulls, flamingoes, gannets, and pelicans.

Darling

The town of **Darling** in the Groenkloof district can trace its origins to 1682, when explorer Oloff Bergh first recorded the lay of the area. As the community developed, farmers began

PREVIOUS PAGES *Stretched out along Langebaan Lagoon are carpets of the West Coast's famed wild flowers. For a few weeks in spring, the blooms provide an unforgettable parade of colour.*

INSET *In thinly populated Namaqualand, local folk still travel as they have always done, and donkey carts like this one are an occasional sight on the roads.*

ABOVE *The West Coast is home to vast colonies of gannets.*

OPPOSITE TOP *Chester the donkey is one of the colourful local characters who delight visitors staying at Club Mykonos.*

OPPOSITE BOTTOM *The splendid Postberg Nature Reserve lies within the West Coast National Park.*

growing vegetables and grain – and even grapes – and keeping dairy cattle. The town eventually became not only a prominent wool-producing centre but also the first area in the country to breed merino sheep. Nearly 200 years after Bergh's initial visit, Lieutenant-Governor of the Cape, Charles Darling – after whom the town is now named – bought Langfontein Farm, and the popularity of Darling escalated.

The **Darling Museum** concentrates largely on the influence of the local dairy industry. Exhibits here include not only replicas of period homes, but displays on the making of butter – wooden churns and washing utensils – and a collection of period dress, furniture and farm equipment.

Naturally it is the spectacle of the flowers that lures most travellers to Darling. The third weekend of September sees the annual **Darling Wildflower Show** – coinciding with the annual **Orchid Show** at the Duckitt Nurseries – which has been prominent on the local calendar for 80 years. Apart from showing the nearly 300 plant species, the show also provides abundant entertainment for visitors to the town. On offer are the seafood dishes and other traditional meals for which the West Coast is famous, market stalls carrying handmade goods, and even a ride on a tractor into the fields of wild flowers. It is here that the lilies, chinkerinchees and bokbaaivygies come into their full glory, interspersed seasonally with golden wheat and lush vineyards.

Not far from Darling is the town of Mamre, where it may be worthwhile to stop off at the museum at the **Mamre Mission Station** – a complex comprising a church, school and watermill. The mission was founded by the German Moravian Missionary Society in 1808. For wine-lovers, a visit to the **Mamreweg Wine Cellar**, just 16 kilometres from the town, is sure to impress. The cellars were established in 1949, and offer wines of exceptional quality and value.

Langebaan

The 17-kilometre-long (10.5 miles) **Langebaan Lagoon, which** lies parallel to the coastline, may be considered the heart of the West Coast, and is particularly rich in birdlife. Archaeological discoveries made here include fossils dating as far back as 10 million years, and a pair of fossilised footprints made by an early human that is estimated to be 117 000 years old.

In the early days of the 20th century, the southern hemisphere's largest whaling station was established on this rugged coast. The lagoon was also the site of the world's largest oyster bed. Today, whaling has made way for gentler pastimes such as fishing, water sports and sailing as holidaymakers flock to Langebaan to escape from the frenetic city life.

The natural splendour of the region is well preserved in the **West Coast National Park**, which protects natural fynbos and one of the most impressive expanses of wetlands in the world.

The original Geelbek homestead, erected in 1860, houses the national park's **Geelbek Environmental and Educational Centre**, where birding facilities include hides and a superb view over the lagoon. The park's **Postberg** segment provides a unique opportunity to spend two days hiking through the veld, and is also home to game and, in spring, more of the region's flowers.

August and September are both good months to see the floral displays, which include gousblom, blombos, tortoise berrybush, strandroos, sea lavender, and wild rosemary of the strandveld fynbos. There are no formal flower shows in the area, but the abundant blooms line all three entry roads into the town.

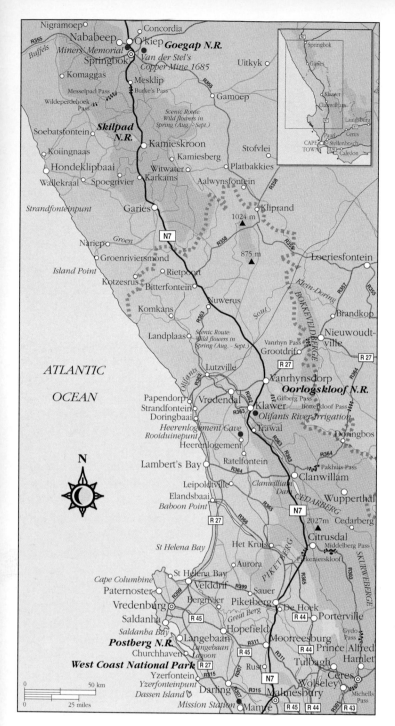

Hopefield

Surrounded by open expanses of renosterveld, rietveld, sandveld and wetlands, the town of **Hopefield** is one of the most picturesque villages on the West Coast. Today, the century-and-a-half-old Dutch Reformed Church is the heart of the town, and a number of the old homes still stand. One of Hopefield's founding families was the Eksteens, who were granted the original **Langrietvlei Farm** by the Dutch governor in 1715. The 1789 manor house, filled with yellowwood and cedarwood and lit by sunlight filtering through the small-paned sash windows, is a national monument. The farm has been presided over since 1834 by the Kotze family, who produce a unique fynbos honey, and also allow hikers and birders access to their wilderness.

The town itself boasts a row of rustic old *hartbeeshuisie* cottages constructed of clay and reeds, which are worth a visit, as is the fascinating **Fossil Museum** on Main Street. The region's fossil history is impressive: Not only did Professor

Langebaan is a centre for horse-riding, sailing, boating expeditions, rides on mules and organised overland trips in four-wheel-drive vehicles. Nearby is the Mediterranean-style resort of **Club Mykonos**. Visitors, however, should try to sample the fresh seafood so widely available here. Undoubtedly one of the most popular eateries – so popular, in fact, that reservations are essential – is the famed **Die Strandloper** restaurant on the edge of the ocean. If you're expecting a plush setting, you're in for a surprise. Die Strandloper is casual and rustic, and the atmosphere is decidedly relaxed. Don't be in a hurry to wolf down your meal. This is the best the West Coast has to offer, and captures the very essence of the unique setting.

Ronald Singer discover Saldanha Man here in 1953, but at Elandsfontein nearby is the site of fossil discoveries that include the remains of sabre-tooth tigers, hippos and the primitive predecessors of today's horses.

Considerably more comfortable than Hopefield's original wattle-and-daub homes is the 18th-century homestead of **Kersefontein**. The farm's current owners have converted the original bakery into a cosy pub, and restored the outhouses on the edge of the Berg River into a comfortable guest chalet.

Naturally, the spring months see plenty of new blooms in the immediate vicinity and the **Fynbos Park Nature Reserve,** and the Hopefield Fynbos Show is held at the end of August every year. Flaming red-hot pokers, flax and erica seem to crowd the verge of the road leading from Hopefield to Velddrif.

Saldanha

The history of **Saldanha** is as old as that of Cape Town, the Mother City. The name of the town and the bay on which it stands comes from the Portuguese admiral, Antonio de Saldanha, and was first given to Table Bay – where the explorer stepped ashore in 1503. The area was home to exiled smallpox victims in the late 19th century, and has been the site of many a shipwreck. When later explorers landed at what is now Saldanha, they simply assumed that the picturesque bay mentioned by de Saldanha was where they too had laid anchor. This same bay was also the first African soil trod by the French Huguenots who settled in the Cape in 1688. More recent times, however, saw a whaling station erected at nearby Salamander Bay, and today the fishing industry is the mainstay of the economy and people of this West Coast town.

Saldanha is an expanding industrial centre, and is the site of an important deep-water harbour for the export of iron ore; tours of the facility are available. Equally important is the natural heritage of the region, which is protected by the **SAS** *Saldanha* **Nature Reserve**. The reserve itself is closed to vehicular traffic, but visitors are welcome to explore the area on foot. To view the fynbos flowers at their best, it is advisable to visit during the six-week period between mid-August and the end of September – especially if you would like to see the buttercup-like *romulea saldanhensis*, endemic to the area.

Paternoster and Beyond

Just 40 kilometres north of Saldanha on Paternoster Bay lies the village of **Paternoster**, an endearing fishing haven consisting of whitewashed cottages. This is getaway country, offering little

more than casual walks on endless beaches, tranquil evenings and the freshest and tastiest crayfish on the subcontinent – the crayfish season extends from November to April. The silence and solitude here is almost divine: the name of the village is Latin for 'Our Father' and echoes the prayers of Portuguese sailors shipwrecked here.

Nearby, at **Cape Columbine**, is the last lighthouse in South Africa that is still tended by a keeper. The tall structure on Castle Rock dates back to 1936, and the Cape Columbine light was usually the first indication of land for ships approaching the southern African coast. The popular Tietiesbaai resort is located nearby, and just three kilometres (1.8 miles) from Paternoster is the **Cape Columbine Nature Reserve**. Established in 1973, the landscape of the reserve consists largely of sandveld – a combination of coastal fynbos and succulents, interspersed with rocky outcrops – which makes it an ideal habitat for birds such as the sacred ibis, as well as gulls and cormorants. The area is open to the public, and features basic camping and caravan stands, but diving for crayfish and *perlemoen* (abalone) is strictly controlled by local authorities.

OPPOSITE *Among the weathered outcrops within the Postberg Nature Reserve is the curious formation known as Finger Rock.*

TOP *The quaint Paternoster Shop serves the distinctly rustic fishing community of Paternoster, north of Saldanha Bay.*

Namaqualand

About 2 000 years ago, early Khoi pastoralists moved onto the land just south of the Orange River, and settled among the granite outcrops on the dry, dusty plains of this desolate area. Today their descendants are known as the Nama, and Namaqualand – named for these people – remains much the same as it was all those years ago, save for the growing numbers of visitors who journey here to view Namaqualand's remarkable seasonal metamorphosis. Despite the blistering arid conditions of this semi-desert, the occasional bouts of good springtime rain bring about a breathtaking transformation, covering the windy flatlands with a vibrant blanket of colourful wild flowers. The revitalized land then takes on an altogether different appearance, with springbok and mountain zebra walking the plains of the floral wonderland.

Although it is known as Namaqualand, the flowering expanse is, in fact, a series of quite small and specific botanic areas stretching northwards to the banks of the Orange River, and includes the Strandveld, the Cedarberg and Olifants River Valley, the Hantam, Sandveld, Knersvlakte, Bokveld, Voor-Bushmanland, Namaqualand Klipkoppe (Hardeveld) and the majestic Richtersveld. The wide expanse of this area is world-renowned for its annual show of flowers, but visitors may find it difficult to cover the entire region. Trips to the Namaqualand area need to be carefully planned to allow for overnight stays and long, tiring hours in a hot car. The villages and nature reserves closer to Cape Town offer every bit of the beauty of the region as a whole, however, and many travellers are content to travel no further than, say, Springbok – in itself a substantial journey.

The Cedarberg and Olifants River Valley

With a relatively high rainfall, the lower reaches of the Olifants River Valley boast a unique variety of plantlife (including the laurel protea and the geelmagrietjie). The fertile lands surrounding towns such as Citrusdal and Clanwilliam are speckled with fields of wheat, fruit orchards and even vineyards. At the same time, however, the less verdant lands are equally beautiful: the lower slopes feature seven-metre-tall (21 feet) waboom trees (*Protea nitida*); the rocky outcrops are home to the rare Clanwilliam cedar tree (*Widdringtonia cedarbergensis*); and the valley's upper slopes feature delicate ericas and leucadendrons. Much of the area is known for its fruit, especially citrus varieties such as oranges, lemons and grapefruit – hence the name of the town of **Citrusdal**, which boasts groves of orange trees, the original seeds of which came from the

Company's Garden in Cape Town. Many of the orchards in the area are open to the public, and visits may be arranged through the local co-operative.

Another important local industry is the rooibos tea plantations centred around the gracious old town of **Clanwilliam**, established in 1732. From Clanwilliam, groups of 15 or more visitors are treated to guided tours of the acres of rooibos (*Aspalathus linearis*) and the sheds where the leaves are processed, and to the flowers of the **Ramskop Nature Reserve** and **Clanwilliam Wild Flower Garden**, and beyond to the Biedouw Valley.

The Wilderness of the Cedarberg

The **Cedarberg Wilderness Area** is watched over by Cape Nature Conservation, and visitors who wish to walk or hike through protected areas such as Sanddrif are required to apply for permits (available at Dwarsrivier). The experience is certain to be a memorable one.

Overshadowed by the 2 030-metre (6 655 feet) Sneeuberg, the famed Clanwilliam cedars of the district are not the only botanical curiosity to be found in the Cedarberg: sharing the mountain wilderness are thickets of wagon trees and a rich array of flowering plants, among them pincushions, disas and other typical fynbos species; the most noted of these is the rare snow protea (*Protea cryophila* or 'cryophila', meaning 'fond of the cold'), found among the fields of snow on the upper reaches and endemic to the area.

The action of rain, snow and cold and water have given the Cedarberg some striking rock formations. Among these are the 20-metre (66 feet) Maltese Cross, the Wolfberg Arch, Wolfberg Cracks – 30-metre (98 feet) clefts in the rockface on Dwarsrivier farm – and the Tafelberg and its Spout. Because of the many streams and waterfalls, conditions here are ideal for the formation of caves, and many of these are adorned with the rock paintings of their early inhabitants. Both the **Stadsaal Caves**, with their maze of passages and chambers, and the **Elephant Cave** at Matjiesrivier boast some fine San rock art. It is easy to understand why the San settled on this land, and why it is so popular with hikers and climbers today, as the Cedarberg

offers astounding views, and a variety of antelope (rhebok, grysbok, steenbok and klipspringer), cats (wild cat and caracal) and other mammals such as baboons and bat-eared foxes, as well as birds ranging from the small sunbirds to majestic birds of prey.

Over the scenic **Pakhuis Pass** from Clanwilliam, the whitewashed cottages of the Moravian Mission at **Wupperthal** preserve the timeless atmosphere of days gone by. Established in 1830, this mission settlement has changed little over the years. The simple roads still see little traffic other than the steady plod of donkeys pulling the carts of the local folk, many of whom work on the tea and tobacco plantations in the district.

The Knersvlakte

Just south of the Namaqualand Klipkoppe, the pebble-strewn hills of the **Knersvlakte** are bordered by the escarpment of the Bokkeveld and Sandveld and the towns of Bitterfontein and Vanrhynsdorp. About 50 kilometres (32 miles) from Vanrhynsdorp is **Nieuwoudtville**, set amid a semi-desert landscape seemingly covered with the fine blooms of the vygie, and annuals such as the botterblom, gousblom, nemesia and beetle daisy. To enjoy the spectacle of flowers, make a point of visiting the starkly beautiful **Oorlogskloof Nature Reserve** over the spring months. The reserve, located on Voortrekker Road

OPPOSITE TOP *The craggy landscape of the Cedarberg is justly renowned for its superb hiking opportunities.*

OPPOSITE BOTTOM *The delicate vygie is among the reasons why Namaqualand is renowned for its annual burst of colour.*

TOP RIGHT *The walls of the Stadsaal Caves display the artistic heritage of the Cedarberg's early inhabitants.*

RIGHT *Even the harshest of environments cannot prevent the wild flowers of the area from showing off their colourful plumage.*

West Coast & Namaqualand

and some fine examples of the rock paintings left behind by the original San inhabitants. From the top of the pass, you can see the green fields of rooibos tea. Where the Matzikama and Koebee mountains join, lie cultivated wheat lands and vineyards that are embellished by the springtime splendour of the wild flowers.

Namaqualand Klipkoppe

Separated from the shoreline by a rocky ridge, the flat plains, formed largely by the Kamiesberg and reaching from Bitterfontein to Steinkopf, are blessed with a bounty of life. Despite its name – Hardeveld means 'harsh lands' – the onset of the rainy season heralds the arrival of Namaqualand daisies and gazanias, interspersed with perdebos, kapokbos and skilpadbos, that seem to carpet the rough valleys here. In the shadow of a crown-shaped mountain stands the town of **Kamieskroon**, whose birth came about when the folk of nearby Bowesdorp deserted their home town – established in 1864 – in favour of a more reliable water source. Although Kamieskroon has grown since its inception in 1924, the only sign of Bowesdorp's existence is the ruins of the original church.

The area is noted for its plentiful flowers, and is home to the **Skilpad Nature Reserve**, just 17 kilometres (11 miles) from Kamieskroon on the Wolwepoort Road. Originally called Skilpadsyferwater for the numerous tortoises that inhabit the wet soils around the seepage holes of the old homestead, the landscape of the reserve comprises mostly shrubs and deserted wheat fields which burst with Namaqualand daisies between July and September. The reserve was established in 1988 by the South African branch of the World Wide Fund for Nature in order to protect the floral heritage and local wildlife – including many small mammals and nearly 100 species of birds. The impressive wilderness here is the main attraction.

about 23 kilometres (14 miles) south of the town, is inaccessible by car, and although the walk from Driefontein can be quite strenuous, the sights that await are reward enough. Baboons, dassies and bat-eared foxes scuttle among the cliffs – watch for black eagles – and the fynbos vegetation is scattered with proteas, gladioli, a variety of sugarbush and the rare *Discorea elephantipes* (or 'elephant's foot'). The Geelbekbosduif Trail also boasts at least nine San rock paintings.

As the northernmost corner of the Cape Floral Kingdom, the 66-hectare (163 acres) **Nieuwoudtville Wildflower Reserve** is home to about 300 different plant species, and bursts into colour during spring when the indigenous geophytes – the world's most prolific – begin to bloom. Through this countryside of Karoo succulents and montane fynbos flows the Doring River, which cascades over the **Nieuwoudtville Falls** to the north of the town and then over the seasonal Maaierskloof Falls. About 7 kilometres (4.5 miles) south of Nieuwoudtville lie the ancient scars left by glaciers 300 million years ago.

On the western side of the Bokkeveld mountains lies **Vanrhynsdorp**, at the foot of the Matzikama Mountains. At the end of Voortrekker Street in the town is the country's biggest succulent nursery and garden, which gives some indication of both the beauty and extent of the unusual plant forms in the area. Floral enthusiasts may choose to walk the 3-kilometre (2 miles) trail through the succulent wilderness at Kwaggaskop, about 30 kilometres (19 miles) to the north of Vanrhynsdorp. On the other side of town, on the other hand, is a marble quarry and one of the country's most productive gypsum mines.

The harsh beauty of the region conceals many surprises. Beyond the **Gifberg Pass** – named after the multitude of hyena poison bushes that are scattered across its face – is a wonderland of protea bushes, small rivers and even a waterfall,

The hamlet of **Garies** – the original Khoi name – in the far south of the Namaqualand Klipkoppe is a small, quiet oasis known for little more than the grasses used to make mattresses, and the fact that the Garies River flows through here en route to the coast, where it empties into the sea as the Groenrivier.

Springbok

The town of **Springbok** – approximately 560 kilometres (350 miles) from Cape Town and 80 kilometres (50 miles) from the coast – began life as a mining settlement in 1685, when VOC governor Simon van der Stel began mining here, having heard of the success the Khoi people had with their primitive copper mines. The last of the shafts sunk by the Dutch governor into the face of what became known as the Koperberg may still be seen near the Goegap Nature Reserve about three kilometres (two miles) from Carolusberg, while the remains of the original smelting works – dating back to the late 1600s – may be viewed at O'Kiep, also the site of the **Nababeep Mining Museum**.

Although only certain sections are open to visitors, the nearby **Goegap Nature Reserve** is a paradise for hikers and naturalists. The reserve is home to aardwolf and Hartmann's mountain zebra, as well as antelope such as gemsbok, eland, klipspringer and springbok – after which the town is named. There are more than 90 species of birds, among them ground woodpeckers, dikkops and birds of prey. Facilities include picnic areas and guided drives among the more than 500 plant species.

OPPOSITE TOP *The Nieuwoudtville Falls present an inviting sight amid the seemingly inhospitable terrain of the region.*

OPPOSITE BOTTOM *Visitors to the town of Springbok may choose to spend the night in an authentic Nama hut.*

ABOVE *As the unofficial capital of Namaqualand, the town of Springbok proudly displays the rich floral heritage of the region.*

USEFUL INFORMATION

WEST COAST INFORMATION

Darling Information Centre (Darling Museum): Pastorie Street, Darling; open Mon-Sat 9am-1pm, 2pm-4pm, Sun 10.30am-1pm, 2pm-4.30pm; tel: (02241) 3361.
Darling Wildflower Show, tel: (02241) 2422/3361.
Flowerline, tel: 082 990 5393/4/5 (calls charged on cellular rates).
Hopefield Fynbos Show: Fynbos Park nature reserve; last week in August (Thurs-Sun); tel: (02282) 3-0856.
Hopefield Tourism Bureau, tel: (02282) 3-0500.
Langebaan Tourism Bureau, tel: (02277) 2-2115.
Saldanha Tourism Bureau, tel: (02281) 4-4484.
West Coast Tourism Bureau: 88 Voortrekker Street, Lamberts Bay; tel: (02281) 4-2088.

PLACES OF INTEREST

Cape Columbine Nature Reserve, tel: (02281) 75-2718.
Club Mykonos: Oliphantskop Road, Langebaan; tel: (02277) 2-2101.
Die Strandloper Restaurant, tel: (02277) 2-2490.
Duckitt Nurseries Orchid Show: 3km from Darling on R307; open May-Nov, first Sat of every month, 9am-12pm; tel: (02241) 2606.
Mamre Mission Station Museum: on R307; tel: (021) 576-1296.
Mamreweg Wine Cellar: on R307; open Mon-Fri 9am-4.30pm, Sat 9am-1.30pm; tel: (02241) 2276/7.
SAS *Saldanha* **Nature Reserve**, tel: (02281) 4-2211.
West Coast National Park, tel: (02277) 2-2144/2798.

NAMAQUALAND INFORMATION

Citrusdal Tourism Office: tel: (022) 921-2181.
Clanwilliam: Publicity/Tourist Division, PO Box 5, Clanwilliam 8135.
Knersvlakte: The Town Clerk, Nieuwoudtville Municipality, PO Box 52, Nieuwoudtville 8180; tel: (02726) 8-1316.
Springbok Information Office: Town Clerk, PO Box 17, Springbok 8240; tel: (0251) 2-2071.

PLACES OF INTEREST

Cedarberg Wilderness Area: Cape Nature Conservation, Citrusdal District Office, Private Bag X1, Citrusdal 7340; open all year 8am-4.30pm; tel: (027) 482-2807.
Goegap Nature Reserve: The Reserve Manager, Goegap Nature Reserve, Private Bag X1, Springbok 8240; guided flower tours; tel: (0251) 2-1880.
Nababeep Mining Museum (O'Kiep Copper Co.): open Tues-Fri, 10am-5pm; tel: (0251) 3-8121.
Nieuwoudtville Wildflower Reserve: Loeriesfontein Road; open July-Oct, 9am-5pm daily; tel: (02726) 8-1052.
Oorlogskloof Nature Reserve: PO Box 142, Nieuwoudtville 8180; open all year 8am-5pm; tel: (02726) 8-1159/1010.
Skilpad Wildflower Reserve (Kamieskroon Hotel): open July-Oct, 8am-5pm; tel: (027) 672-1614; Flower walks: PO Box 30, Kamieskroon 8241, tel: (0257) 762.

West Coast & Namaqualand

Southern
Cape Coast

Excursion Five

Southern Cape Coast

The southern coastline of the Western Cape is a delightful mix of cultures, attractions and unsurpassed natural splendour. Each of the communities – ranging from lively holiday resorts to sleepy little towns – along these shores has its own charm, while the waters offshore are an important whale breeding ground. At Cape Agulhas – the southernmost point of the African continent – the waters of the Indian and Atlantic oceans meet.

Strand and Gordon's Bay

Located on the eastern shores of False Bay, **Strand**'s white sands – 'strand' means 'beach' – make it ideal resort territory, and the holiday season usually sees the beaches packed with visitors. Much of this small but modern town caters for visitors, and the idyllic climate makes it that much more attractive. The Strand promenade, with its popular restaurant, juts right out into the ocean and boasts a splendid view of both the sea and the surrounding mountain. Sailboats skim the waves, children frolic on the white sand and sunbathers swim and soak up the sun. Surfers, however, tend to prefer either Koeëlbaai or Gordon's Bay to the southeast.

Pinpointed by the giant 'GB' marked out on the slope of the mountain, the resort town of **Gordon's Bay** has come a long way from its early days as a simple fishing harbour. Today it boasts one of the country's finest yacht clubs and a number of impressive holiday developments along its coast. The harbour, however, still evokes its modest past: casual fishermen cast their lines from the harbour wall or from small boats, and boats may be hired to fish the deeper waters. The two beaches here cater for the specific needs of holidaymakers. As its name suggests, Bikini Beach is the domain of sun-worshippers, while Main Beach is reserved largely for active watersports.

Hangklip to Kleinmond

Initially a whaling station, the small town of **Betty's Bay** was established as a somewhat exclusive getaway spot in the early 1930s. It is still a relatively quiet holiday location but, like many other communities on this coast, is particularly popular over the end-of-year holiday season.

Despite the resort atmosphere, this part of the Cape coast also caters for nature lovers. Disa Kloof at the nearby **Harold Porter National Botanic Gardens** on the mountain slopes, for

---

PREVIOUS PAGES *Backed by a rugged offshoot of the Hottentots-Holland Mountains, Clarence Drive winds along the scenic eastern shore of False Bay from Gordon's Bay to Pringle Bay.*

PREVIOUS PAGE INSET *Undoubtedly the most thrilling of sights in spring is the breeching of southern right whales off Hermanus. The whales come here in spring to bear their young.*

ABOVE *Hermanus's official Whale Crier, Pieter Claasen, welcomes Maurice Jones, a town crier from Farford in the United Kingdom.*

OPPOSITE TOP *A Gordon's Bay chandler's shop manifests the town's longstanding link with the sea.*

OPPOSITE BOTTOM *Strand's beach is a magnet for sailors.*

instance, is a natural paradise, with a magnificent stream and waterfall, and a multitude of wild flowers, including the disa. Just as enchanting is **Stony Point Reserve**, about 188 hectares (465 acres) of mostly montane fynbos, and the first nature reserve to be declared on the southern African subcontinent. The vivid red disa is particularly prevalent over December, and the reserve is also a breeding sanctuary for jackass penguins. If the fynbos vegetation is of special interest, be sure not to miss out on the display at the **Kogelberg Conservation Area**, located near Kleinmond and about 10 kilometres (6 miles) east from Betty's Bay. The reserve, and especially its Kogelberg Trail, is most noted for its splendid show of fynbos – about 20 per cent of fynbos species are found here – but there is also plenty of small wildlife to view, including antelope and numerous bird species. Canoeing is permitted on the Palmiet River, which forms one of the borders of Kleinmond, a small coastal town tucked between the Palmiet and the Bot rivers. The surrounding fynbos-covered mountainside is also ideal for hikers, as is the **Kleinmond Coastal Nature and Mountain Reserve**. The 1 000-hectare (2 470 acres) reserve is home to more than 1 500 indigenous plant species, including the endemic *Erica pillansii*, and alsothe micro frog – the world's rarest amphibian. Hiking trails cover both the confines of the reserve and the adjoining Kleinmond Lagoon.

Hermanus

During the holiday season, **Hermanus** bustles with holidaymakers, but off-peak periods are considerably more sedate. The seaside town ranks as one of the Cape's most popular getaway spots, and accommodates visitors from near and far. The relatively new harbour now houses a modern clubhouse and a variety of boats and watersport equipment, including windsurfers and paddle-skis – popular pastimes along this stretch of the southern Cape coast. Sunset cruises from the harbour are a perennial favourite with holidaymakers. The accent in Hermanus is most definitely on having fun: hang-gliders and paragliders soar overhead; the town is dotted with pubs, restaurants, stylish cafés and braai spots; and, of course, the beaches teem with bikini-clad bathers, surfers and sun-worshippers. The largest and most popular stretch of sand is Grotto Beach, which stretches past the Klein Rivier Lagoon to Die Plaat.

A favoured Hermanus hangout is the clifftop path overlooking Walker Bay, the country's top whale-watching spot. This vantage point is presided over by the world's only official whale crier, whose job is to alert the public – he carries a horn made of kelp – that whales have been spotted in the bay. For this purpose, he now carries a cellphone to keep his followers abreast of the migration patterns and movements of the whales. A number of tour guides operating in the Walker Bay area now offer visitors the chance to descend in underwater cages to see great white sharks – now a protected species in South African waters – off Hermanus.

Because the seas off Hermanus form part of the marine reserve, divers who wish to brave the ocean either to explore or search for seafood delicacies are obliged to purchase permits from the magistrate's office on Main Road. For the less adventurous, there is plenty to see on land. Apart from the seals which tend to congregate in the area, the view from the top of the cliff overlooking the Old Harbour is quite spectacular, and the harbour itself offers a number of fascinating diversions. Old fishing boats – some dating back to the mid-1800s – are on permanent display here, and there is also a Harbour Museum telling the story of the local whaling and fishing industry. Exhibits include part of a whale skeleton and seawater tanks

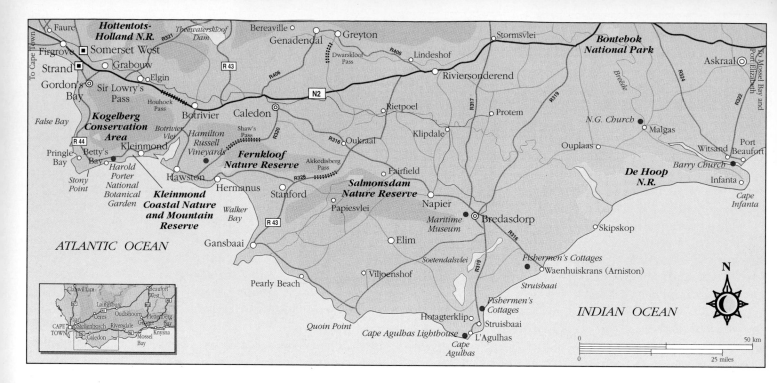

brimming with the plant and animal life found out to sea. For the benefit of whale-watchers, telescopes have been set up above the Old Harbour – there are also coin-operated ones on Village Square – and sonar equipment allows visitors to hear the calls of the whales off the coast.

At the foot of the harbour cliffs stands the Perlemoen Hatchery where abalone are bred – either to be released (in order to maintain the indigenous population) or sold to the specialised abalone 'farmers' in the region. Appointments may be made to tour the operation.

Covering much of the area inland from Hermanus, the 1 550-hectare (3 830 acres) **Fernkloof Nature Reserve** stretches from Maanskynbaai to Hemel-en-Aarde valley and boasts a 60-kilometre (37 miles) network of excellent walking trails – demarcated and colour-coded according to difficulty and length – through coastal and montane fynbos terrain. The reserve features ericas, proteas and over 1 000 other plant species (many of which may be seen on display at the visitors' centre). More than 100 bird species frequent the reserve, and mammals such as baboons and small antelope are quite

common. Fernkloof's Spring Wildflower Show usually takes place in September, at about the same time as the annual Whale Festival, a community celebration involving a variety of entertainment in a convivial atmosphere.

The people of Hermanus, however, do not depend on the seasonal visitors, and the town has developed a number of small industries of its own. Many of the country's most prominent painters and artists live and work in and around Hermanus, and there are numerous craft shops, galleries and flea markets where visitors can purchase locally produced items.

Because of the town's location, its many restaurants naturally emphasise local seafood. There are a number of popular eateries in and around the centre of town, many of which boast impressive views over the ocean. Topmost among these are the upmarket **Marine Hotel** (à la carte menu and carvery), **Nautilus** (seafood) and the intriguing **Bientang's Cave**, which nestles in the base of the cliff overlooking the beach and is

thought to be the original home of Bientang, the last indigenous Strandloper ('beach walker') of these parts. Booking at most of these venues is essential.

Wine-lovers should certainly not forget to stop at the celebrated **Hamilton Russell Vineyards**, set in the picturesque Hemel-en-Aarde valley in the mountains of Glen Vauloch on the fringe of the town. The vineyards are quite spectacular, and visitors can sample some of the estate's fine wines.

Stanford to Arniston

The little village of **Stanford**, on the banks of the Klein River, is rich in both history and rural atmosphere, and offers a more tranquil lifestyle than resort towns such as Hermanus. Here, visitors may take boats and canoes out onto the river, amble

---

OPPOSITE *The panoramic Old Harbour of Hermanus is now a museum, and boasts extraordinary views of Walker Bay.*

ABOVE *The fishing village of Waenhuiskrans is also called Arniston, after a British troopship that sank here in 1815.*

RIGHT *Fishing is an important industry in and around Arniston, and local delicacies include dried fish.*

the most famous spot along this shoreline: L'Agulhas and the famed **Cape Agulhas Lighthouse**, erected in 1848. Cape Agulhas is Africa's southernmost tip and the confluence of the two oceans, but it is also one of the most treacherous stretches of coast on the continent, known locally as the Graveyard of Ships. The lighthouse is open to the public and has a coffee shop and small museum.

Just beyond Agulhas is the small resort town of **Struisbaai**, a 14-kilometre (9 miles) strip of pristine beach said to be the longest in the southern hemisphere. The name of the village is taken from the many ostriches which once roamed the land here. (The Afrikaans word for ostrich is *volstruis*.) Although considered by many as lost in time, the little hamlet offers weary travellers the opportunity to catch their breath by either fishing off the rocks or taking a relaxing pleasure cruise. Virtually the entire shore is dotted with historic fishermen's cottages, which reach as far as **Arniston**. This popular retreat, with its thatched cottages and snow-white sands, was traditionally a fishing village. The quaint community was originally known as Waenhuiskrans (meaning 'wagon house cliff'), after the great cavern overlooking the beach a short walk to the southwest of the village.

through the fynbos vegetation and watch the plentiful birdlife that inhabits the district. In fact, a favourite bird-watching spot is the nearby **Salmonsdam Nature Reserve**, where an array of bird species flit about the montane fynbos and over the breathtaking mountains and vales.

Gansbaai, on the other hand, remains a traditional fishermen's village, complete with rustic old cottages and fishing fleets. Modern progress has allowed for the development of a new harbour, and a fishing factory has also been established in the vicinity. Fortunately, these changes have not detracted from the tranquil beauty of this charming little bay, and – like Struisbaai to the east – Gansbaai is a favoured getaway for many Capetonians. The most prominent natural feature of this stretch of shoreline is the 8-kilometre (5 miles) 'peninsula' known as Danger Point. The most famous victim of this jagged coastline was HMS *Birkenhead*, a British troopship that ran aground on 26 February 1852 on the rock which has now taken its name. More than 400 men lost their lives on that fateful night, which gave rise to the Birkenhead Drill – the principle of 'women and children first'. Tours of the memorial and lighthouse may be arranged with the local Information Office.

To the south lies the aptly named **Pearly Beach**, a peaceful strip of sparkling sand popular among anglers and divers who visit Dyer Island – with its colony of penguins – just off the coast. A little further along the coast from Pearly Beach is probably

De Hoop Nature Reserve

Although the **De Hoop Nature Reserve** is not accessible from Arniston – the nearest access point is at Ouplaas and a considerable journey – to miss out on the reserve would be a pity, especially for bird-watchers. The magnificent 40-kilometre (25 miles) shoreline boasts a marine reserve extending 5 kilometres (3 miles) out into the Indian Ocean – both swimming and diving are allowed – and a 14-kilometre (9 miles) lagoon simply teeming with over 250 bird species. Many waders and nearly all South Africa's water birds are found here, as well as species such as the Damara tern, the Cape vulture and the black oystercatcher. Apart from the prolific birdlife, a number of mammal species may also be spotted here, among them bontebok, eland, rhebok, springbok, duiker, Cape mountain zebra, baboon, grey mongoose, caracal, and the endangered Cape clawless otter. There is a fascinating diversity of plant life – about 50 of De Hoop's 1 500 plants are endemic – including the Bredasdorp sugarbush.

Watching the Whales

Although the **Western Cape Whale Route** actually starts as far away as Lambert's Bay on the West Coast, it is the southern Cape coast which is traditionally the best spot to see the whales cavorting in the ocean with their young. Because of the popularity of this natural spectacle, at least 45 special information boards have been posted at various locations along the route, providing enthusiasts with details on the visiting species and their most favoured spots.

Although the calving season may begin as early as June – the humpbacks start migrating from about May and Bryde's whales are seen virtually throughout the year, albeit further out to sea – the months between August and November will almost guarantee a sighting. Southern right whales are attracted by the warmer waters and abundance of food, and it is here that they give birth to their young and nurse them until the calves are strong enough to travel. Whale-watchers flock to the shores of Stony Point near Betty's Bay, Kleinmond, Onrus, De Kelder and Koppie Alleen in the De Hoop Nature Reserve, but viewing boats are forbidden to approach within 300 metres (915 feet) of the whales. The most popular spot to see the animals, however, is at Hermanus, the very centre of the Whale Route, and one of the best sites for whale-watching in the world.

OPPOSITE TOP *Cape Agulhas is Africa's southernmost tip, and the point where the Atlantic and Indian oceans meet.*

OPPOSITE BOTTOM *The welcoming beacon of the Agulhas lighthouse has long guided mariners past this treacherous coast.*

ABOVE *Visitor accommodation at De Hoop Nature Reserve is styled along the classic lines of local vernacular architecture.*

RIGHT *Cycling is just one way to appreciate the diversity and unspoiled environment of De Hoop.*

USEFUL INFORMATION

Arniston (Waenhuiskrans) Information Office, tel: (02841) 4-2584.
Cape Nature Conservation (booking office): Private Bag X1, Uniedal, 7612; tel: (021) 889-1560 (Jonkershoek).
Cape Overberg Tourism Association: PO Box 250, Caledon, 7230; tel. (0281) 4-1466.
Gansbaai Information Office (tours), tel: (02834) 4-1439.
Hermanus Tourism Bureau, tel: (028) 312-2629.
Stanford Information Office, tel: (028) 341-0340.
Struisbaai Information Office, tel: (02841) 4-2584.
Suidpunt Publicity Association, PO Box 51, Bredasdorp 7280; tel: (028) 414-2584.
Whale hotline, tel: 0 800 228 222.
Whale Crier, tel: 083 212 1075.
White Shark Ecoventures, tel: 082 658 0185; **White Shark Tour**, tel: (02834) 4-1380;

PLACES OF INTEREST

Arniston Hotel, tel: (02847) 5-9000.
Cape Agulhas Lighthouse (Soetendalsrand Nature Reserve), open Tues-Sat 9.30am-4.45pm, Sun 10am-1.30pm; tel: (02841) 4-2584.
Fernkloof Nature Reserve (by appointment), tel: (028) 313-0300.
Harold Porter National Botanic Garden, tel: (02823) 4010; horse-riding, tel: (02823) 3141.
Kleinmond Coastal Nature Reserve, (hiking trails), tel: (02823) 2-9363/4010.
Kogelberg Conservation Area, open daily 7.30am-5pm; tel: (02823) 2-9425.
Perlemoen Hatchery, Hermanus, tours by appointment; tel: (028) 312-2140.
Rooiels Nature Reserve, tel: (02823) 2-9363.
Salmonsdam Nature Reserve, tel: (028) 341-0789.

153

The Garden Route

Excursion Six

The Garden Route

The scenic splendour that is the Garden Route has been heralded as the Cape's finest treasure, and a visit to this 230-kilometre (140 miles) stretch of sparkling sands, rugged cliffs, wild flowers and sleepy inland waters will testify to this tribute. The roads that lead from Mossel Bay to the Tsitsikamma forests are shielded by the Outeniqua and Tsitsikamma mountain ranges, lined with a breathtaking array of lagoons and lakes, coves and cliffs, and lapped by the warm waters of the Indian Ocean. The Garden Route shelters a fascinating diversity of plant and animal life, and is also a leisure playground – with attractions such as water-skiing, boating, diving, paragliding, fishing, swimming and surfing.

Mossel Bay

The Garden Route starts officially at **Mossel Bay**, a small but well-established resort town 390 kilometres (240 miles) from Cape Town. Blessed with balmy summers and moderate winters, the beaches of this seaside town have long been a favoured holiday spot. For a glimpse of what the town offers, visit in June when the Food and Wine Festival is held.

By the time Bartolomeu Dias first visited the picturesque cove in 1488, the area we know today as Mossel Bay had already been settled by Strandlopers – a nomadic clan of Khoi who travelled the beaches of the Cape living on what was offered by the ocean, including the mussels for which the bay is named. Mossel Bay has seen considerable development since the Portuguese explorer set foot here. The streets are lined with many national monuments, and the town enjoys an enviable reputation for the fine seafood caught nearby. In recent years, the extraction of offshore gas and oil deposits has brought considerable development to the town.

Mossel Bay's charm stems from its colourful history and maritime influence – commemorated at the annual **Dias Festival**. In 1988, to mark the 500th anniversary of the Dias expedition, the **Bartolomeu Dias Museum** was established, and its satellite museums and monuments – the Maritime Museum, Munro's Cottages and the Dias Cross – are popular drawcards. One of the most intriguing sights is the famed **Post Office Tree**, a giant old milkwood where sailors would leave letters to be collected by the next ship heading for home.

PREVIOUS PAGES *The scenic splendour of Wilderness entirely justifies the name of the Garden Route.*

PREVIOUS PAGE INSET *The thriving ostrich farms of Oudtshoorn offer a fascinating diversion along the Garden Route.*

ABOVE *Mossel Bay's Bartolomeu Dias Museum chronicles more than 500 years of maritime history.*

OPPOSITE TOP *The magical qualities of the Cango Caves attract many thousands of sightseers each year.*

OPPOSITE LEFT *Girded by quiet gardens, George's Dutch Reformed Church watches over the town.*

OPPOSITE RIGHT *Mossel Bay's Dias Monument is dedicated to the Portuguese mariner who was the first European to set foot here.*

Mossel Bay is closely tied to the sea, and many visitors are drawn by its marine life. Whales and dolphins may be sighted beyond the breakers – The Point is a good vantage spot – and jackass penguins and seals may be seen throughout the year. In fact, a number of operators offer harbour cruises, which take sightseers and nature lovers to the shores of **Seal Island**, the home of a colony of nearly 2 000 seals.

Ostrich Country

Enclosed by the mountains of the Outeniqua and Swartberg ranges, the town of **Oudtshoorn** is the seat of the Little Karoo's 'ostrich kingdom'. Oudtshoorn is dotted with monuments and museums, including the **CP Nel Museum**, with its period furniture and ostrich mementoes and the **Cango Caves Museum**. The town is perhaps most renowned for its 19th-century 'feather palaces' – extravagant manor houses erected by wealthy ostrich farmers at the height of the feather boom – and as the home of the magnificent **Cango Caves**, located about 30 kilometres (19 miles) north of the town. Carved by water dripping through layers of limestone rock, the spectacular chambers and dripstone formations attract thousands upon thousands of visitors every year. Consisting of a series of winding passages and soaring chambers held aloft by towering pillars, the Cango Caves are among the most impressive in the world. The largest of the caverns is Van Zyl's Hall, a mammoth chamber over 100 metres (330 feet) long, 55 metres (180 feet) wide and 17 metres (56 feet) high. There are few formations within these stone walls that do not inspire awe, including the dripstone Organ Pipes, Cleopatra's Needle and the Frozen Waterfall. Access to this important heritage site is now strictly regulated to preserve the caves in their natural state. Sadly, vandals have already left their mark, and the lights erected for better viewing have resulted in the growth of moss and algae. There are three kilometres open to public exploration; visitors who take one of three hourly tours are requested to abide by the rules.

For those who wish to see Africa's wildlife, a visit to the **Cango Crocodile Farm** and **Cango Wildlife Ranch** is a must. More than 400 alligators and crocodiles are bred here for research purposes. Although criticised by some for caging wild animals, such as lions, cheetahs, leopards and the exotic jaguar and puma, the park-like operation is a genuine attempt to educate the public, many of whom may never have the opportunity to see these creatures in their natural habitat. In fact, the ranch is the headquarters of a very successful cheetah breeding project, and visitors are invited to view and photograph the animals from the safety of a walkway running above the enclosures. The farm also has a popular reptile house, otter pond and pens housing pygmy hippos and a pack of endangered wild dogs.

No visit to Oudtshoorn would be complete without an encounter with the birds

that made the town famous. Three of the 400 local ostrich farms – **Highgate**, **Safari**, and **Cango Ostrich and Butterfly Farm** – have been opened to the public. Visitors may ride on the backs of these giant birds, visit the breeding stations and hatcheries, and purchase ostrich plumes, eggs, meat (including biltong) and leather products. An exciting alternative is to take a ride on the **Ostrich Express**, a train journey through the semi-arid Little Karoo, which ends at a wine farm in Calitzdorp. Guests are wined and dined before retiring in comfort, to be railed back to Oudtshoorn in the morning.

George

Named for King George III, this historic centre of the Garden Route lies in the shadow of the lush Outeniqua Mountains, surrounded by the natural glory with which the district has become synonymous. The landscape around **George** is one of bountiful rivers, prosperous farmland and colourful flora. Together with neighbouring Heroldsbaai, Wilderness and Sedgefield, the town is an extremely popular leisure stop for fishermen, anglers and watersport enthusiasts.

Housed in the town's old courthouse, the **George Museum** is an excellent place to explore local heritage – make a point of seeing the collection of old gramophones. The museum also tells the story of the local timber industry, which is based on the

LEFT *The breathtaking Outeniqua Pass connects George with the town of Oudtshoorn in the Little Karoo.*

OPPOSITE *The Outeniqua Choo-Tjoe crosses the mouth of the Kaaimans River on its route between George and Knysna.*

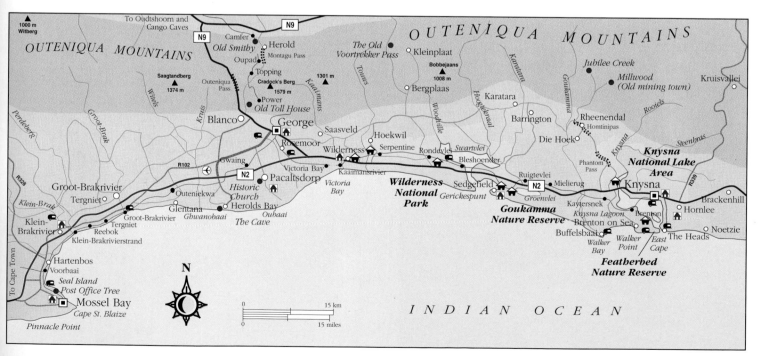

indigenous forests in the vicinity. To view a selection of the fine yellowwood and stinkwood products manufactured here, visit the local factories or the outlet in York Street.

Equally integral to the town's character are its many houses of worship – not for nothing was George known as Cathedral City. The most impressive features are the domed ceiling of the **Dutch Reformed Church**, the stained-glass windows of **St Mark's Cathedral**, and **St Peter and St Paul**, the oldest surviving Catholic church in South Africa.

Sporting pursuits are well catered for here. George is home not only to two excellent golf courses – **Fancourt Country Club** boasts a championship course – but there is also the local

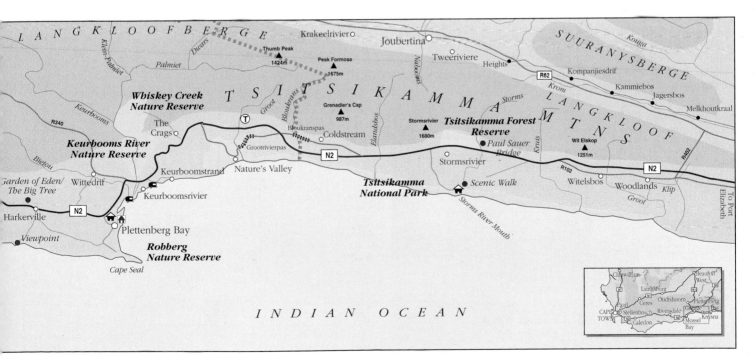

riding club, the George Sports Club, and a number of favourite watersport venues: safe swimming and surfing at Victoria Bay; waterskiing at Rondevlei and Swartvlei; snorkelling at Gericke's Point; bass fishing at Lake Pleasant; and fishing spots stretching from Glentana through to Plettenberg Bay.

A relatively new development quite close to town is George's own crocodile park, a small research facility which not only breeds crocodiles, but is also home to a variety of indigenous bird species.

Running between George and Knysna is the rail line which carries the **Outeniqua Choo-Tjoe**, a train pulled by a vintage steam engine dating back to 1893. The line follows a spectacular route along the coast, and is a popular mode of transport for visitors who wish to sit back and enjoy the experience rather than face the prospect of a car journey. The train leaves George just after 8am daily; some 3½ hours later, after crossing the bridge over the famed Knysna Lagoon, the Outeniqua Choo-Tjoe pulls into its destination – and departs for George again at about 1pm.

The Wilderness Lakes Area

As its name suggests, the Wilderness area is precisely that – a great stretch of unspoilt terrain at the foot of the Outeniqua mountains. This is the setting for the **Wilderness National Park**, a 10 000-hectare (24 700 acres) spread incorporating Wilderness Lagoon, the Touw River estuary, the Rondevlei and Swartvlei lake system and part of Groenvlei, which forms the border with the Goukamma Nature Reserve to the west – and bounded in the south by the Indian Ocean. This natural haven caters for nature lovers, who flock to the area: whale-watchers, horse-riders, bird-watchers (about 200 bird species may be spotted from the hides within the park, about 80 of which are water birds) and the many sport lovers who hang-glide, parasail and hike here – especially popular is the 12-kilometre (7.5 miles) **Kingfisher Trail**.

With its spectacular natural forests and wildlife, nearby **Sedgefield** is an equally popular retreat which offers much the same sorts of diversion as Wilderness. The tranquil waters here are edged with beds of reeds and sedges – from which the town gets its name – and the wildlife, attracted by the bountiful source of food and shelter, is equally prolific. Gericke's Point, popular among spear-fishermen, boasts some fascinating rock formations, and just as interesting is the water life of Swartvlei, a saltwater lake which is ideal for swimming and other water-based leisure activities.

Adjoining the fishing paradise of Groenvlei – also known as Lake Pleasant – is the **Goukamma Nature Reserve** and the adjacent marine reserve. Goukamma incorporates just over 2 000 hectares (4 940 acres) of largely coastal fynbos vegetation, with a network of more than 35 kilometres (22 miles) of trails, ranging from 4-kilometre hikes (taking about 1½ hours) to 14 kilometres (about 5 hours). A number of watersports are permitted, although permits are necessary to

ABOVE *Wilderness National Park's rest camps offer the tranquillity suggested by the park's name.*

LEFT *Like many of the old-fashioned farmstalls of the district, Knysna's Elephant Walk Farm Stall offers homemade delicacies.*

OPPOSITE *The craggy Heads form a narrow entrance to the peaceful holiday playground of Knysna Lagoon.*

fish the waters of the reserve. The flora and fauna are important drawcards: over 200 bird species have been recorded here, and Goukamma is home to both the common and blue duiker, vervet monkeys, the Cape grysbok and bontebok. The latter is found in protected areas of both Goukamma and Wilderness National Park, closed to the public for conservation reasons. The splendour of the Wilderness Lakes region, however, does not end with Sedgefield but extends to the Buffalo Bay and Walker Point – both favourite holiday destinations – and beyond to Brenton-on-Sea.

Knysna

The 'beautiful land' – as depicted on its coat of arms – is indeed a gift of the gods. Of all the enchanting spots along the Garden Route, the finest must be the **Knysna National Lake Area**, a spectacularly unspoilt expanse that includes the town of Knysna, the surrounding forests, the lagoon and the rocky Knysna Heads which guard this sanctuary. Because it is one of the country's favourite holiday and tourist destinations and situated on South Africa's biggest and most valuable estuary, the area is closely monitored by conservationists. Other reasons to safeguard the area include the over 36 000 hectares (89 000 acres) of indigenous forests, which contain mostly yellowwood and stinkwood, and Knysna Lagoon's oyster farming operations – visit in July to sample the fresh seafood at the annual Knysna Oyster Festival. The area is also home to some unique species which have now become synonymous with Knysna: the pansy shell, the Knysna loerie and Knysna seahorse.

The town itself is part of the original property owned by George Rex, a man of mystery and legendary character who lived here in the early 1800s and is said to have been an illegitimate son of George III. None of the tales have ever been proven, but they do add to the romantic charm of the town. Today a small yellowwood structure houses the **Knysna Museum**, which not only tells the story of Rex, but also displays the history of the modern town. The building originally stood on the site of the country's first gold diggings at **Millwood**, some 25 kilometres (16 miles) north-west of Knysna, and currently being redeveloped to restore it to its former glory.

Although Knysna has its share of modern shopping complexes, many of its century-old houses are now occupied by the small art and craft shops and industries for which Knysna is known. One such place is **Reitzer's Soap Worx**, which stocks handmade glycerine soaps and aqueous cream cosmetics.

The Knysna Lagoon has recently seen the development of **Knysna Quays**, a waterfront development catering largely for the recreation of visitors. Although colourful and vibrant, it is rather more expensive than the facilities offered within the town and has been accused of detracting from the natural aesthetics of the area and jeopardising the local environment.

Leisure activities abound in the area, and range from bird-watching and hiking – there are many demarcated trails in the local forests, including the famous 100-kilometre (62 miles), eight-day **Outeniqua Hiking Trail** – to scenic drives and guided drives through local game farms. Because of the easy access to the lake and the sea, watersports are plentiful and

Beacon Island has now made way for an impressive hotel complex, and the lagoon and beaches crawl with holidaymakers. Central Beach is the venue for the annual World Hobie Championships.

For those seeking the quieter pleasures, the Robberg and the Keurbooms River nature reserves are ideal getaways. The 175-hectare (432 acres) sandstone promontory that is the **Robberg Nature Reserve** juts about 4 kilometres (2.5 miles) into the sea. Much of this area has been declared a marine reserve, so permits are required (available at the entrance). The furthest point of the reserve is known as Cape Seal – the term 'robberg' means 'seal mountain' – because of the hundreds of seals that lived here when Khoi Strandlopers walked these shores. Robberg is a breeding ground for seabirds, including cormorants, gulls and oyster-catchers. The **Keurbooms River Nature Reserve** to the north-east of the town adjoins both the Keurbooms River State Forest and the Whiskey Creek Nature Reserve, home of the Plettenberg Bay Angling Club. The atmosphere here is relaxed, and activities centre on fishing, watersports and bird-watching.

include canoe trips, diving and cruises on the lagoon. Visitors may also hire houseboats, and the *John Benn* entertains guests as they cruise the quiet waters.

Accessible only via the Featherbed Ferry or by private boat, the **Featherbed Nature Reserve** sprawls across the slopes of the western Head, at the entrance to the lagoon. The 70-hectare (173 acres) reserve is geared largely toward conservation, with educational tours for schools and other special-interest groups concentrating on the ecology of the region. The terrain covered by the reserve also includes hiking trails: the 2.2-kilometre (1.2 miles), one-hour Bushbuck Trail, and a 5-kilometre (3 miles) trail along a more scenic and less strenuous route. All hikes must be led by an approved guide.

Plettenberg Bay

The landscape around Tsitsikamma and Plettenberg Bay comprises about a dozen conservation areas – there are more plant varieties here than in the entire northern hemisphere – and marine reserves. At the same time, the area depends on seasonal visitors, so much is made of the blessings of nature, with plenty of horse-riding routes, waterways for canoeing and trails reserved for hikers.

With its pristine beaches, sparkling waters and emerald forest backdrop, Plettenberg Bay is still one of South Africa's premier and most fashionable leisure spots. The area was first settled by Portuguese sailors stranded here after the *São Gonçalo* foundered off the coast here in 1630 – Ming porcelain recovered from the wreck forms part of the Jerling Collection at the town's municipal offices. A whaling operation situated on

162

Tsitsikamma

The fynbos and forests of the Outeniqua and Tsitsikamma are undoubtedly the Cape's most beautiful, and are exceptionally rich in wildlife – especially birds, which number over 280 different species. The area is blessed with a high rainfall and water is integral to the ecology of the region: Tsitsikamma's name stems from the Khoi word for the sound of running water, the source of the Storms River is in the high wetlands and the landscape is laced with mountain streams.

The **Tsitsikamma National Park** stretches for approximately 80 kilometres (50 miles) along the coast and extends about 5 kilometres (3 miles) out into the Indian Ocean, enclosing a precious marine reserve that is home to dolphins, whales and an array of seashore life. Qualified scuba divers can follow underwater trails to view the sealife first hand, but the experience onshore is equally rewarding. The landscape, including the adjacent state forest reserve with its giant Outeniqua yellowwoods, assegaai and other tree species, is home to indigenous flora such as orchids and lilies. The forests are home to common mammals such as baboon, duiker and grysbok, and even the rare Cape clawless otter, after which the popular 50-kilometre (31 miles) **Otter Trail** is named.

In addition to the Otter Trail, there are a number of other walks and hikes within the confines of the national park, state

---

OPPOSITE TOP *Popular Plettenberg Bay is a favoured resort of fun-seekers and holidaymakers.*

OPPOSITE BOTTOM LEFT *The beautiful Knysna loerie is an unofficial symbol of the Garden Route.*

OPPOSITE BOTTOM RIGHT *Over many aeons, ocean waves have helped carve formations such as Cathedral Rock at Keurbooms.*

ABOVE *Lined with age-old yellowwood trees, the Outeniqua Trail features high on the destination list of hikers.*

USEFUL INFORMATION

De Hoek Circuit Hiking Trail, tel: (044) 279-1829.

Knysna Hiking Trails, tel: (044) 382-5466.

Knysna Oyster Festival, tel: (044) 382-1610.

Knysna Tourism Bureau Publicity Association, tel: (044) 382-5510.

Mossel Bay Marketing: cnr Market/Church roads, Mossel Bay; tel: (044) 691-2202.

Oudtshoorn Publicity Association: Voortrekker Road, Oudtshoorn; tel: (044) 272-2221/279-2532.

Outeniqua Choo-Tjoe: Rex Street, Knysna; tel: (044) 382-1361; Station Street, George; tel: (044) 801-8288.

Outeniqua Hiking Trail, tel: (044) 882-5466.

Ou Tol Circuit Hiking Trail (Swartberg Pass), tel: (044) 272-7820.

Rovos Rail (Garden Route: Cape Town-Knysna), tel: 421-4020.

Sedgefield Information Bureau: PO Box 882, Sedgefield; tel: (044) 343-2658.

PLACES OF INTEREST

Cango Caves Museum: call for directions; tel: (044) 272-7410.

Cango Crocodile Farm and **Cango Wildlife Ranch**: Baron Van Reede Street, Oudtshoorn; open daily 8am-5.30pm; tel: (044) 272-5593.

Cango Ostrich and Butterfly Farm, tel: (044) 272-4623.

CP Nel Museum: 3 Baron Van Reede St, Oudtshoorn; tel: (004) 272-7306.

Featherbed Nature Reserve (hiking trail), tel: (044) 382-1693.

Gamka Mountain Reserve (Tierkloof Trail, Pied Barbet Trail), tel: (044) 213-3367; Nature Conservation tel: (044) 279-1739 .

George Museum: York Street, George; open Mon-Fri 9am-4.30pm, Sat 9am-12.30pm; admission free; tel: (044) 873-5343.

Goukamma Nature Reserve (trails): Sedgefield; tel: (044) 382-0042.

Highgate Ostrich Show Farm, tel: (044) 272-7115.

Itulu Game Farm: PO Box 2308, George; tel: (044) 871-1289.

John Benn **Pleasure Boat** (for hire), tel: (044) 382-1693.

Knysna Angling Museum: Queens St., Knysna; tel: (044) 382-6138.

Knysna Museum: Queen Street, Knysna; tel: (044) 382-5066.

Plettenberg Bay Tourism, tel: (044) 553-4065.

Reitzer's Soap Worx: cnr Clyde/Long streets; tel: (044) 382-5797.

Safari Ostrich Show Farm, tel: (044) 272-7311.

Spring Street Gallery: 19 Spring St., Knysna, tel: (044) 382-5066.

Tsitsikamma National Park, PO Box Storms River; tel: (042) 541-1607.

Wilderness National Park: PO Box 35, Wilderness; tel: (044) 877-1197.

---

forest and the adjoining de Vasselot area. But, after a trip along the Garden Route, travellers may choose to put their feet up at Nature's Valley, a charming village and reserve at the foot of the Groot River Pass. Virtually enclosed by the tall trees and lush woods of the Tsitsikamma forest and surrounding mountains, it is an ideal setting to catch your breath and unwind.

The Garden Route

DIRECTORIES

Shopping · Cuisine · Nightlife · Events

Shopping

Cape Town is considered by many to be the shopping mecca of South Africa, and the city has all sorts of shopping experiences to tempt you. Like much of South Africa, Capetonians are spending more and more time and money bargain-hunting at flea markets and roadside stalls rather than at the established department stores and retail outlets. The city's current explosion of development has meant higher and higher turnover for everything from shopping malls to designer boutiques and even grocery stores.

Naturally, many of the tourist attractions, from the most obscure to the most visited, have their own 'in-house' shops, selling curios, souvenirs, crafts and books.

The pavements of many business districts, such as the city centre and suburbs such as Claremont, Wynberg, Muizenberg, Fish Hoek and others, are lined with open-air markets which stock an assortment of goods – usually at very reasonable prices. The items here tend to be mass-produced, but there are also stalls selling African crafts such as wire toys, soapstone busts, wooden statuettes, beadwork, basketware and woven goods. Although it is virtually impossible to tell whether these have been made by entrepreneurial locals or within the confines of a local 'factory' – in fact, many originate in Zimbabwe and other neighbouring countries – they are probably handmade, and do represent indigenous African handcrafts.

Antiques

Because it is the oldest European settlement in southern Africa, Cape Town tends to be the country's antique capital. Many of the genuine articles – and certainly the real bargains – may be found in small, out-of-the-way dealers who do not, in fact, cater for the antique market at all. Of course, with the influx of bargain-hunters and the realisation that there is a demand for old Cape furniture, Victorian jewellery, and old china, prices are rising, and many dealers are cashing in. Nevertheless, shoppers are sure to find at least one piece worth buying.

Some of the most popular hunting grounds are what has become known as the 'Antique Market' along the pavements of Church, Burg and Long streets in the city centre; the Main Road of Kalk Bay, especially **Aladdin's Cave**, 76b Main Road, Kalk Bay, tel: 788-8882, and **Cries of London**, 82 Main Road, Kalk Bay, tel: 788-3256; and along Main Road, which winds through the southern suburbs from Woodstock, Observatory and Mowbray through Wynberg, Diep River and beyond.

ABOVE *The bountiful farmlands outside the city furnish local vendors with plenty of tempting fresh produce.*

OPPOSITE *A modern office tower dwarfs a picturesque antique store at the corner of Long and Church streets.*

Antique dealers include **Julian Adler Antiques & Africana**, Loop Street, tel: 422-1901; **Antiques on Kloof**, 167 Kloof Street, Gardens, tel: 423-6280; **Bruce Tait Antiques**, Buitenkloof Centre, Kloof Street, Gardens, tel: 422-1567; **The Cape Workshop**, 196 Main Road, Diep River, tel: 712-3239; **Clarewoods Antiques & Interiors**, Vineyard Road, Claremont, tel: 683-4839; **The Junk Shop**, 206 Long Street, tel: 424-0760; **Kaapse Draai**, 329 Voortrekker Road, Parow, tel: 92-1716; **Oudeschuur**, 8 Kildare Road, Wynberg, tel: 761-2075; **Stephan Welz & Co**, 86 Hout Street, Cape Town, tel: 423-4728; **Peter Visser Antiques**, 117 Long Street, Cape Town, tel: 230-7870; **Yesteryears & Tomorrows**, 7 Cavendish Street, Claremont, tel: 671-9366.

Art

Much like elsewhere, quality contemporary art is expensive in Cape Town, and visitors are advised to buy through reputable art dealers, such as: **Alpha Fine Art**, corner Anreith/Hans Strijdom Ave, Cape Town, tel: 418-2320; **Alfred Mall Gallery**, 9a Alfred Mall, V&A Waterfront; tel: 419-9507; **The Cape Gallery**, 60 Church Street, Cape Town, tel: 423-5309; **Chelsea Gallery**, 51 Waterloo Road, Wynberg, tel: 761-6805; **Everard Read Gallery**, 6226 Victoria Wharf, V&A Waterfront, tel: 418-4527; **Die Kunskamer**, Saambou Building, 14 Burg Street, Cape Town, tel: 424-4238.

At the same time, however, there are a number of local outlets for talented artists who may not have the clout to exhibit in upmarket galleries or be represented by the top art dealers. Most of the informal art-and-craft markets so prolific over summer weekends on the peninsula sell the work of budding artists, and so do the more popular outdoor markets such as **Greenmarket Square**, **St George's Mall**, **Green Point Market** (on the periphery of Green Point Stadium), **Kirstenbosch Craft Market**, the **Hout Bay Market**, **Art-in-the-Park** on Silwood Road in Rondebosch, and on the verge outside the **Constantia Nek Restaurant** in Constantia. There are many smaller galleries dotted around the Cape – such as those along the **Kalk Bay Main Road** – that exhibit local artists. One of the most worthwhile to visit if you're up the West Coast is the **West Coast Gallery**, in Velddrif, tel: (02288) 3-0942/1118. Also worth a few hours of the art-lover's time is a tour around the popular **Noordhoek Art Route**, tel: 789-1328.

Important local collections may be seen at: the **South African National Gallery**, Government Avenue, Gardens, tel: 465-1628; the **Natale Labia Museum**, 192 Main Road, St James, tel: 788-4106; **Rust-**

en-Vreugd, 78 Buitenkant Street, Cape Town, tel: 465-3628; **Old Town House** (Michaelis Art Collection), Greenmarket Square, Cape Town, tel: 424-6367; **Irma Stern Museum**, Cecil Road, Rosebank, tel: 685-5686; **Sasol Art Museum**, tel: 808-3695; **University of Stellenbosch Art Gallery**, tel: 808-3489; **Rembrandt van Rijn Art Museum** (Libertas Parva), tel: 886-4340.

Books

Ask any Capetonian where to buy reading matter and you'll likely be directed to Long Street in the city centre, home to some of the most famous bookstores in the country. Top of the list is **Clarke's Bookshop**, 211 Long Street, Cape Town, tel: 423-5739, followed by the **First Edition Book Café**, 159 Long Street, Cape Town, tel: 424-7650; **Africana Books**, tel: 461-2382; **Select Books**, 186 Long Street, Cape Town, tel: 424-6955. Other book dealers include **The Caxton Bookshop**, 278 Main Road, Kenilworth, tel: 762-1613; **Bookwise**, 195 Long Street, Cape Town, tel: 423-1504; **Corner Bookstore**, 216 Long Street, Cape Town, tel: 424-4503; **ID Booksellers**, Westminster House, 122 Longmarket Street, Cape Town, tel: 23-9104; **Reader's Den**, 148 Long Street, Cape Town, tel: 424-9027. For second-hand books, try **The Book Nook**, 31 Main Road, Heathfield, tel: 712-9610; **Book Treasures**, 148a Main Road, Sea Point, tel: 434-4329; and **Cafda Bookshop** (Werdmuller Centre, Main Road, Claremont, tel: 674-2230; Mimosa Arcade, Regent Road Sea Point, tel: 434-6149). Be sure also to visit the flea markets and other informal markets, such as Greenmarket Square, the Grand Parade and many others, which stock used and old books at very low prices indeed.

The main bookselling chains represented in Cape Town are: **Exclusive Books** (Cavendish Square, Claremont, tel; 674-3030; Constantia Village, Spaanschemat Road, Constantia, tel: 794-7800; 225 Victoria Wharf, V&A Waterfront, tel: 419-0905); **CNA** (**Central News Agency**; head office, tel: 54-1261/7181); **PNA** (head office, tel: 914-5570); **Wordsworth Books** (544 Tyger Valley Centre, Bellville, tel: 914-1346; Gardens Centre, Gardens, Cape Town, tel: 461-8464). Naturally, the curio shops at all the top tourist spots, such as Table Mountain, Kirstenbosch Botanical Gardens and others, stock publications covering the destination itself and related topics.

Clothing

As the home of the country's garment industry, the Cape Peninsula boasts many clothing outlets, ranging from the designer wear of exclusive boutiques to the casual wear – and more – from the factory shops which abound in the semi-industrial suburbs of Salt River and Woodstock. For a comprehensive list of these factory outlets – although all boast 'factory prices', not all keep their promise – consult Pam Black's *A-to-Z of Factory Shops*, published by the author herself and available at most bookshops. Although factory shops tend to concentrate in less-accessible industrial areas, Main Road is lined with an endless variety of shops, many of which sell only clothing. These may range from the fashionably expensive to the cheaper lines aimed at the general populace, but there are a few gems worth visiting,

including many secondhand stores. Among the latter are the timeless classics of beaded gowns, fur jackets, crocheted shawls, embroidered bags, and silk gloves of **Secondhand Rose**, 28 Main Road, Claremont, tel: 674-4270; **Deja Vu**, 278 Main Road, Kenilworth, tel: 797-7373; and **Second Time Around**, 196 Long Street, Cape Town, tel: 423-1674. Both new and secondhand clothes may be bought at the local markets – Greenmarket Square, Constantia, Kirstenbosch, Cape Town Station, Hout Bay. If you're looking for fabric, don't miss the ocean of materials available at the **Grand Parade** in Darling Street, and the **Oriental Plaza** on the corner of Sir Lowry and Oswald Pirow roads, or visit **Mnandi Textile & Design**, 90 Station Road, Observatory, tel: 447-6814. Most of the informal markets sell mostly handcrafted garments, but if this is your taste, then make a point of visiting the small boutiques and craft outlets along Main Road in Hout Bay, especially **Africa Nova** (Main Road, Hout Bay, tel: 790-4454). You'll find handmade garments at both the **Blue Shed** (the Waterfront Craft Market) and the **Red Shed** at the V&A Waterfront; look for the exquisite jackets of **Solveig**. Remember, too, that many of the small towns in the Western Cape, and particularly those that serve rural communities, boast many outlets selling homemade clothes, many of which are of very good quality. One such place is **Le Cott Gifts & Decor**, Verster Street, Paarl, tel: 872-5479.

If, however, you're more at home with the designer look, the city is not only home to many of the country's premier couturiers, but also to a wide selection of exclusive fashion salons. Many are concentrated around the plush shopping malls such as **Cavendish Square** in Claremont, the **Tyger Valley Centre** in Bellville and the **Constantia Village** centre in Constantia. At the same time, however, don't ignore the established chain stores as many represent some of the big fashion names of Europe and the US, including Calvin Klein, Diesel, Levi Strauss, and other sought-after brand names. A good bet, too, is the **Young Designers' Emporium** (Waldorf

Building, St George's Mall, Cape Town, tel: 424-1514; Cavendish Square, Claremont, tel: 683-6177), a cooperative venture providing an outlet for the talents of new young designers on the fashion front. The high-fashion stores are lavish caverns lined wall-to-wall with designer names, but there are also the less ostentatious outlets which stock casual attire and sportswear at very reasonable prices.

To hire fancy dress and costumes – and even evening wear – there is really only one reputable dealer in Cape Town: call **Sue Farmer Costumes and Tux Hire** (55 Morningside, Pinelands, tel: 531-1919; 16 Voortrekker Road, Bellville, tel: 949-5782).

Crafts, Curios and Souvenirs

Cape Town is filled with crafts and curios representing the indigenous people of the subcontinent. Some are authentic, some aren't; some are exquisite, and some of very poor quality; some are outrageously expensive, others remarkably cheap – and all may be found at upmarket curio shops, middle-of-the-road souvenir outlets, and informal roadside stalls.

The peninsula's plethora of flea markets – at Constantia, Kirstenbosch, and Hout Bay, for example – all sell indigenous crafts, as do the established markets at Greenmarket Square and Green Point Stadium. Informal roadside stalls, such as those near Adderley Street and on the fringe of Cape Town railway station, also sell curios and – alongside their own souvenir series – so do the city's popular tourist attractions, such as Kirstenbosch, Table Mountain, Groot Constantia, Mariner's Wharf in Hout Bay and, of course, the **Blue Shed** (Waterfront Craft Market, tel: 418-2850) and the **Red Shed** at the V&A Waterfront (V&A Visitors' centre, tel: 419-9429/418-2369). Other opportunities to buy local crafts, curios and souvenirs may be had at **Masephumelele Village**, Main Road, Kommetjie, tel: 387-5351; **Imhoff's Gift**, Kommetjie Road, Kommetjie, tel: 790-2730; **The Chapman's Bay Trading Centre**, corner Beach Road/Pine Street, Noordhoek, tel: 789-1788; **African Art**, 83 Redhill Road, Simon's Town, tel: 780-9904; **African Souvenirs**, Market House, 5 Greenmarket Square, Cape Town, tel: 423-8008; **African Image**, 57 Burg Street, Cape Town, tel: 423-8385. **Elephant Walk**, 48 Strand

ABOVE *Cape Town's hawkers have brought the shopping experience from the malls to the streets.*

OPPOSITE *Taking pride of place among the city's many malls is the handsome Victoria Wharf at the V&A Waterfront.*

Street, Cape Town, tel: 419-6219; **Indaba Curios**, Cavendish Square, Claremont, tel: 671-9306; **Induna Village**, 90 Main Road, Kalk Bay, tel: 788-1603; **Out of Africa**, 125 Victoria Wharf, V&A Waterfront, tel: 418-5505; **Springbok Curios & Gems**, 251 Victoria Wharf, V&A Waterfront, tel: 425-1807.

The smaller towns outside the peninsula also have Saturday-morning craft markets, and specialised curio outlets: **Clementina Ceramic Studio**, on the R303, Paarl, tel: 872-3420; **Dombeya Farm**, corner Annandale/Strand roads, Stellenbosch, tel: 881-3746; **Jean Craig Pottery**, Devon Valley Road, Stellenbosch, tel: 883-2998; **Kleinplasie Complex**, on the Robertson Road, Worcester, tel: (0231) 2-2225/6.

If you are looking for gems and traditional African jewellery, visit the markets and jewellers in most of the shopping malls, or any of the craft and curio outlets listed above, but see also **Afrogem**, 64 New Church Street, Cape Town, tel: 424-8048.

Markets

Probably the most popular shopping venue in South Africa is the market: flea market, craft market, street market, fish market and produce market. Like much of the country, Cape Town has its fair share of informal stalls and kiosks lining the pavements of the city and suburbs, and filling virtually every possible stretch of open ground over weekends.

The most renowned of the city's informal market places is the **Grand Parade** on Darling Street – rows upon rows of fabrics, garments, haberdashery and trinkets – and **Greenmarket Square**, an eclectic collection of secondhand goods, trendy fashion, collectibles and junk. Weekends see a mushrooming of

similar markets: the bric-a-brac stalls of the **Green Point Market** alongside the Green Point Stadium; the arts and crafts of **Art-in-the-Park** in Rondebosch; **Kirstenbosch Craft Market**; the handmade goods on **Hout Bay's Main Road**; **Muizenberg Pavilion**; **Jubilee Square** in the heart of Simon's Town; and the garments available on **Cape Town Station** daily.

The markets at the **V&A Waterfront**, however, are extremely popular, and visitors and locals alike flock there to sift through the goods of the **Red Shed**, the **Waterfront Craft Market** in the Blue Shed, and the fresh produce available in the **King's Warehouse**. Prices here tend to cater for tourists who benefit from the favourable exchange rate, so if you're looking for bargains, you may decide to visit the less lavish markets which have become commonplace in the city streets.

Neighbouring towns, however, also tend to offer much along the lines of casual weekend markets. Stellenbosch boasts the **Winelands Craft Market** (every Sunday during summer); Paarl has its own flea market (off Main Street), and an **Art and Craft Market** (in Victoria Park on the first Saturday of the month), as do other towns in the vicinity, such as Worcester, Hermanus, Langebaan, and others.

Shopping Malls

Considering its modest size in relation to the shopping meccas of Paris, New York, Rome, London, Singapore and even Johannesburg, Cape Town boasts an array of sophisticated department stores and an equally impressive number of shopping malls. All the larger business centres have at least one complex devoted to the shopping experience, generally anchored by one or more of the leading department or chain stores. Although some of the smaller neighbouring towns are somewhat limited in variety, Saturday mornings see malls buzzing with regular shoppers. The busiest shopping malls are **Cavendish Square** (Claremont, tel: 674-3050); **Victoria Wharf** (V&A Waterfront, tel: 418-2369); **Riverside Shopping Centre** (Main Road, Rondebosch, tel: 685-4442); **Constantia Village**, (Constantia, tel: 794-5065); **Blue Route Mall** (Tokai, tel: 713-2061); **St George's Mall** (city centre, tel: 25-3440); **The Gardens Shopping Centre** (Gardens, Cape Town, tel: 465-1842); **The Alfred Mall** (V&A Waterfront, tel: 419-9429/418-2369); **The Link** (Claremont, tel: 674-2180); **Maynard Mall** (Wynberg, tel: 797-1714); **Kenilworth Centre** (Kenilworth, tel: 671-5054); **The Arcade Shopping Centre** (Fish Hoek, tel: 782-6112). There is an enormous number of smaller, more intimate shopping centres, many of which house most of the country's most popular department and chain stores.

Cuisine

Traditional Fare

For the best traditional Cape meals, visitors should consider the upmarket eateries of Constantia. Rated among the country's finest restaurants are **Buitenverwachting** (Klein Constantia Road, Constantia, tel: 794-3522) and **Constantia Uitsig** (Spaanschemat River Road, Constantia, tel: 794-4480).

Restaurants with an African theme include: **Africa Café** (Lower Main Road, Observatory, tel: 447-9553); **Bayfront Blu Restaurant and Coffee Bar** (Two Oceans Aquarium complex, V&A Waterfront, tel: 438-2650); **Blue Plate** (35 Kloof Street, Gardens, tel: 424-1515); **De Volkskombuis** (Aan de Wagenweg, Stellenbosch, tel: 887-2121); **Emily's** (77 Roodebloem Road, Woodstock, tel: 448-2366); **Kaapse Tafel** (90 Queen Victoria Street, Cape Town, tel: 423-1651); **Mama Africa** (178 Long Street, Cape Town, tel: 424-8634); **Shebeen on Bree** (25 Bree Street, Cape Town, tel: 421-7139). For true Cape Malay cooking, try **Cape Manna** (tel: 419-2181).

On the popular wine estates, restaurants of note are the **Traditional Cape Kitchen** at Blaauwklippen (tel: 880-0133/4) and the **Vintner's Platter Restaurant** at Delheim (tel: 882-2297) on the Stellenbosch Wine Route. Also highly regarded are **Boschendal** (Pniel Road, Groot Drakenstein, tel: 874-1252) and the **Lanzerac Hotel** (Stellenbosch, tel: 887-1132).

Fast Foods

Eat-on-the-run meals are easy to come by in Cape Town. **Victoria Wharf** and the **King's Warehouse** on the V&A Waterfront have plenty of takeaway joints, and vendors sell their wares (often *samoosas* and other traditional finger foods) at the Grand Parade and at all the street markets throughout the city. Similar outlets are also found at the more popular beaches and in shopping malls. Watch for **McDonald's**, **Kentucky Fried Chicken**, **Nando's Chicken**, **King Pie**, **Steers**, **Marcel's Frozen Yoghurt**, **St Elmo's Pizzaway** and **Something Fishy**.

Seafood

For the best of the Cape's superb fish and seafood, try the following: **Black Marlin** (Main Road, Miller's Point, tel: 786-1621); **Blue Peter's Upper Deck** (Blue Peter Hotel, Popham Road, Bloubergstrand, tel: 554-1956); **Brass Bell** (Main Road, Kalk Bay, tel: 788-5455); **Burgundy** (Market Square, Hermanus, tel: (0283) 22-800); **The Musselcracker** (Victoria Wharf, V&A Waterfront, tel: 419-4300); **Panama Jack's** (Quay 500, Cape Town Harbour, tel: 447-3992); **Die Strandloper** (Beach Road, Langebaan, tel: (02287) 2-2490); and **Mariner's Wharf** (Hout Bay Harbour, tel: 790-1100).

Cafés and Bistros

Cape Town has its fair share of both upmarket and casual bistros: **Caffé San Marco** (Victoria Wharf, V&A Waterfront, tel: 418-5434); **Hemingways** (90 Strand Street, Cape Town, tel: 419-6534); **Inter Mezzo** (Nico Theatre Centre, DF Malan Street, Cape Town, tel: 418-6418); **Natural Café** (Victoria Junction, 63 Prestwich Street, Green Point, tel: 419-9797); **Drum Cafe** (32 Glynn Street, Gardens, tel: 461-1305); **Senhôra Sardine** (105 Lower Main Road, Observatory, tel: 448-1979); **Obz Café** (115 Lower Main Road, Observatory, tel: 448-5555).

Popular Eateries

Many of the trendiest restaurants have unique attractions. Some are fashionable, while others simply offer fine food in an exquisite setting. Reservations are essential at the following: **The Funky Food Emporium** (corner Belvedere/Keurboom roads, Claremont, tel: 683-0127); **Gardener's Cottage** (Montebello Estate, 31 Newlands Avenue, Newlands, tel: 689-3158); **Jackson's** (Peninsula Hotel, 313 Beach Road, Sea Point, tel: 439-8302); **Jake's** (5 Summerley Road, Kenilworth, tel: 797-0366); **Morton's on the Wharf** (Victoria Wharf, V&A Waterfront, tel: 418-3633); **Hard Rock Café** (Victoria Wharf, V&A Waterfront, tel: 418-0222); **Caffé Balducci** (Victoria Wharf, V&A Waterfront, tel: 421-6002); **The Courtyard** (Vineyard Hotel, Colinton Road, Newlands, tel: 683-3365); **De Goewerneur** (Castle of Good Hope, Castle Street, Cape Town, tel: 461-4895); **Two Oceans** (Cape Point, tel: 780-9200); **Blues** (The Promenade, Victoria Road, Camps Bay, tel: 438-2040); **Kronendal** (Main Road, Hout Bay, tel: 790-1970); **Planet Hollywood** (Dock Road, V&A Waterfront, tel: 419-7827); **Cantina Tequila** (V&A Waterfront, tel: 419-8313); **Hatfields** (129 Hatfield Street, Gardens, tel: 465-7387); **Café Bardeli** (Longkloof Studios, Darters Road, Cape Town, tel: 423-4444); **Suikerbossie** (Victoria Drive, Hout Bay, tel: 790-1450).

For Oriental or Indian cuisine, try **Fortune Garden** (Beach Road, Sea Point, tel: 434-8188); **Mr Chan** (178a Main Road, Sea Point, tel: 439-2239); **Sukhothai** (50 Orange Street, Gardens; tel: 423-4725); **Gaylord's** (65 Main Road, Muizenberg, tel: 788-5470); **Kotobuki** (3 Avalon Centre, Mill Street, Gardens, tel: 462-3675); and **Perima's** (Belvedere Road, Claremont, tel: 671-3205).

Top Restaurants

A number of restaurants combine exceptional cuisine, fine service and a magnificent setting. The best of the best include: **Cape Colony** (Mount Nelson Hotel, 76 Orange Street, Gardens, tel: 423-1000); **Champers** (Deer Park Drive, Vredehoek, tel: 465-4335); **Chez Michel** (Main Road, Franschhoek, tel: 876-2671); **Clementine's** (Wolfe Street, Wynberg, tel: 797-1053); **Floris Smit Huis** (55 Church Street, Cape Town, tel: 423-3414); **La Maison de Chamonix** (Chamonix Estate, Uitkyk Street, Franschhoek, tel: 876-2494); **Bonthuys** (121 Castle Street, Cape Town, tel: 426-2368); **Bosman's** (Grande Roche Hotel, corner Plantasie/Constantia roads, Paarl, tel: 863-2727); **Parks** (114 Constantia Road, Wynberg, tel: 797-8202); **Le Quartier Français** (16 Huguenot Street, Franschhoek, tel: 876-2151); **La Petite Ferme** (Pass Road, Franschhoek, tel: 876-3016)

Mediterranean

Many local menus concentrate on the rich, filling food of the Mediterranean: **Max Max** (Kloof Street, Cape Town, tel: 24-1424); **Café Paradiso** (110 Kloof Street, Gardens, tel: 23-8653); **Dias Tavern** (Portuguese) (27 Caledon Street, Cape Town, tel: 45-7547); **Piazza Trevi** (Constantia Village Shopping Centre, Constantia, tel: 794-5065); **Fascination Café** (BMW Pavilion, V&A Waterfront, tel: 419-5850 ext 235); **Aldo's** (Italian) (Victoria Wharf, V&A Waterfront, tel: 421-7874); **La Perla** (Italian), (Beach Road, Sea Point, tel: 434-2471); **Anatoli** (Turkish) (24 Napier Street, Cape Town, tel: 419-2501); **Ari's Souvlaki** (Greek) (83a Regent Road, Sea Point, tel: 439-6683); **Maria's** (Greek) (32 Barnet Street, Gardens, tel: 461-8887); **Quay West** (Cape Grace Hotel, West Quay, V&A Waterfront, tel: 418-0520).

OPPOSITE *An established favourite among Capetonians is the sumptuous Italian cuisine of La Perla in Sea Point.*

TOP *Pulsating music and live sports broadcasts are among the drawcards of the Waterfront's vibey Sports Café.*

Out of the Ordinary

Top among dining alternatives are: **New York Bagels** (corner Regent/Clarens roads, Sea Point, tel: 439-7523), a collection of separate food stalls (for which you pay by means of a unique 'smart' card system); **Teacher's Spirit of Adventure** (Alfred Basin, V&A Waterfront; tel: 419-3122), a floating restaurant berthed at the V&A Waterfront; and, overlooking Table Bay, **Top of the Ritz** (Ritz Hotel, Rhine Road, Sea Point, tel: 439-6010), the city's only revolving restaurant.

Fresh Food and Delicatessens

For the finest fresh produce, try the **King's Warehouse** at the V&A Waterfront and, for fish, **Willoughby & Co** (Victoria Wharf, V&A Waterfront, tel: 418-6116); **Kalk Bay Harbour** and **Mariner's Wharf** in Hout Bay for fish and seafood; the **Old Cape Farmstall** (corner Main/Constantia roads, Constantia, tel: 794-7062) and **Oakhurst Farm Stall** (tel: 762-1827).

The Cape's finest delis include: **Belvedere Farm Stall** (Belvedere Road, Rondebosch, tel: 683-9018); **Carlucci's** (corner Upper Orange/Montrose Ave, Oranjezicht, tel: 465-0795); **Emilio's Food Store** (31 Breda Street, Oranjezicht, tel: 461-9304); **Giovanni's** (Main Road, Green Point, tel: 434-6893); **Oakhurst Deli Shoppe** (Summerley Road, Kenilworth, tel: 762-1539); **Pasta Freddi** (Cavendish Close, Claremont, tel: 683-2085); **Riese's** (Main Road, Sea Point, tel: 434-3465).

Wine

As the heart of the country's wine industry, the Cape and its winelands offer an almost unlimited number of outlets for fine wines. Apart from the estates of Stellenbosch, Paarl, Franschhoek and even Constantia, try city stockists such as **Vaughan Johnson's Wine Shop** (Market Square, V&A Waterfront, tel: 419-2121); **Steven Rom Exporters** (Sea Point tel: 439-6043); the **Olde Wine Shoppe** (Mariner's Wharf, Hout Bay, tel: 790-1100); **Oom Samie's Fine Wine Library** (84 Dorp Street, Stellenbosch, tel: 887-2612), and the **Wine Warehouse** (Ravenscraig Road, Woodstock, tel: 448-2371).

169

Nightlife

Pubs, Bars and Taverns

Whether it's after a long day at the office or a hot day on the beach, Capetonians flock to the city's many pubs and bars – and end up staying until the wee hours, especially if it's Friday. Some of the most popular city venues are: **The Rockin' Shamrock** (39 Loop Street, Cape Town, tel: 419-5255); **Perseverance Tavern** (83 Buitenkant Street, Cape Town, tel: 461-2440); **The Set** (Victoria Junction Hotel, Green Point, tel: 418-1234); **On the Rocks** (Ambassador Hotel, Victoria Drive, Bantry Bay, tel: 439-6170); **Villamoura** (The Promenade, Victoria Road, Camps Bay, tel: 438-1850); **Quay Four Tavern** (Quay 4, V&A Waterfront, tel: 419-2008); **Sports Café** (Victoria Wharf, V&A Waterfront, tel: 419-5558); **Cranzgot's** (Harbour Road, Hout Bay, tel: 790-3160); **The Big Blue** (Harbour Road, Hout Bay, tel: 790-5609); **Groot Constantia Tavern** (Groot Constantia Estate, tel: 794-1144); **Peddler's on the Bend** (Spaanschemat River Road, Constantia, tel: 794-7747); **Ferryman's** (East Pier Road, V&A Waterfront, tel: 419-7748).

There are also a number of British- and Irish-style pubs in the **O'Hagan's**, **Keg**, and **McGinty's** chains.

Theatre

Cape Town's theatres present a variety of dramatic, comic, dance and musical production. The main theatre venues are the **Baxter Theatre Complex** (Main Road, Rosebank, tel: 685-7880); **Nico Theatre Centre** (DF Malan Street, Cape Town, tel: 410-9800); **Theatre on the Bay** (Links Street, Camps Bay, tel: 438-3301); **Maynardville Open-air Theatre** (corner Church/Wolfe streets, Wynberg). There are also a few community theatres dotted around the suburbs. Book seats for all these venues though Computicket (tel: 430-8000).

Music

All the city's theatres host music recitals ranging from classical to popular and, occasionally, traditional music. Watch the daily press for details on what is showing at: **City Hall** on Darling Street, Cape Town; **Agfa Amphitheatre** at the V&A Waterfront; the **Oude Libertas Amphitheatre** and the **Spier Open-Air Amphitheatre** in Stellenbosch.

For fine jazz, try the **Green Dolphin Restaurant** (Alfred Mall, V&A Waterfront, tel: 421-7471); and **Dizzy's Jazz Café** (Camps Bay Drive, Camps Bay, tel: 438-2686). Bookings for most music recitals may be done through Computicket.

Cinema

All the major shopping malls have at least three or four cinemas showing the very latest Hollywood releases and, occasionally, acclaimed foreign films. The major cinema chains are Ster-Kinekor and Nu-Metro, and the biggest venues are the **Blue Route Mall**, Retreat; **Maynard Mall**, Wynberg; **Kenilworth Centre**, Kenilworth; **Cavendish Square** and **The Atrium**, Claremont; **The Golden Acre**, city centre; **Victoria Wharf**, V&A Waterfront; **Tyger Valley Shopping Centre**, Tyger Valley. The intimate three-screen **Labia Theatre** (68 Orange Street, Gardens, tel: 245-927) is also worth a mention. Bookings for all movies may be made through Computicket.

The top cinematic experience is the world-famous **IMAX Cinema** at the BMW Pavilion on Portswood Road in the V&A Waterfront. This is the world's largest film format, and is projected onto a five-storey screen. Screening times are on the hour, and screenings last roughly an hour (tel: 419-7364).

Gambling

Gambling is illegal in South Africa (except at licensed casinos) and, at the time of writing, no casinos operate legally in the Cape Town area. The only permitted form of gambling is horse racing, and there are tracks in Kenilworth and Milnerton. Contact the **Western Province Racing Club** for more information (tel: 762-7777).

Nightclubs

Cape Town is notorious for its rather erratic club life. The booming holiday season from November to February usually sees a plethora of new clubs – nearly all of which are forced to close their doors as autumn nears. Although the city centre buzzes until the small hours, most revellers patronise pubs and bars rather than all-night dance clubs. There are, however, favourites which attract a loyal clientele. Among them are **Arena**, **Elusion**, **Orange** and **Shebeen on Bree**. Be sure to watch the daily press for new clubs and one-off party extravaganzas which tend to be very popular over the festive season.

Cabaret

Venues devoted to cabaret are few in Cape Town, with most of the limited performances moving from small, intimate restaurants to established theatres. Establishments which concentrate on traditional cabarets include **The Harbour Theatre** (Kalk Bay) and **On Broadway** (21 Somerset Road, tel: 418-8338). Watch the daily press for up-to-date news on these events.

Safety

As in all big cities, the night brings the need for vigilance. Cars parked in the centre of town may be a particular risk, so always lock your car, and never leave valuables inside. Park in a well-lit area or in a pay-as-you-park facility, and never walk alone to your car after dark. In an emergency, call the **flying squad** on 10111 for police assistance, and report any serious incident, such as a mugging, car accident or assault as soon as possible.

OPPOSITE *As they near the finish line of the gruelling* Cape Argus-Pick 'n Pay Cycle Tour, *held each year in March, cyclists pass palm-fringed Camps Bay Beach.*

Events

JANUARY
• New Year Coon Carnival (2 January)
• Opening of Parliament

FEBRUARY
• Community Chest Carnival, Maynardville
• J&B Metropolitan Handicap, Kenilworth
  Race Course

MARCH
• The *Cape Argus*-Pick 'n Pay Cycle Tour
• Nederburg Wine Auction, Paarl

APRIL
• Franschhoek Festival
• Two Oceans Marathon
• Crayfish season ends

MAY
• Whale-watching season starts
• Snoek season starts

JUNE
• Snoek Festival, Hout Bay

JULY
• Knysna Oyster Festival
• Snoek season ends
• Namaqualand flower season starts

AUGUST
• Hout Bay Festival
• Namaqualand flower season at its best

SEPTEMBER
• Whale-watching season at its peak
• Darling Wild Flower and Orchid Show
• Stellenbosch Festival
• Sparkling Wine Festival, Paarl
• Fernkloof Spring Wildflower Show, Hermanus

OCTOBER
• Stellenbosch Food and Wine Festival

NOVEMBER
• Crayfish season starts

DECEMBER
• Rothmans Week Yacht Racing, Table Bay

INDEX

Page numbers in **bold** indicate photographs.

Index